Heaven & Beyond

Also written by the authors

Angelspeake: How to Talk with Your Angels
The Angelspeake Book of Prayer and Healing
The Angelspeake Storybook

Heaven & Beyond

*Conversations with
Souls in Transition*

Barbara Mark
and Trudy Griswold
authors of *The Angelspeake Storybook*

Published by
Adams Media Corporation
260 Center Street, Holbrook, MA 02343. U.S.A.
www.adamsmedia.com

ISBN: 1-58062-478-2

Printed in Canada

J I H G F E D C B A

Library of Congress Cataloging-in-Publication Data
Mark, Barbara.
Heaven and beyond / by Barbara Mark & Trudy Griswold.
p.   cm.
ISBN 1-58062-478-2
1. Spiritualism. 2. Death--Miscellanea.
I. Griswold, Trudy. II. Title.
BF1275.D2 M37   2001
133.9--dc21   00-050250

This publication is designed to provide accurate and authoritative information with regard to the subject matter covered. It is sold with the understanding that the publisher is not engaged in rendering legal, accounting, or other professional advice. If legal advice or other expert assistance is required, the services of a competent professional person should be sought.
— From a *Declaration of Principles* jointly adopted by a Committee of the American Bar Association and a Committee of Publishers and Associations

Some names have been changed to protect the privacy
of the individuals involved.

Every effort has been made to secure permissions for the
poems and excerpts appearing in this book.

Cover photograph ©Orion Press/Natural Selection Stock Photography

This book is available at quantity discounts for bulk purchases.
For information, call 1-800-872-5627.

This book is gratefully dedicated to

Bob Griswold
A truly spiritual man

Thank you for your constant,
generous, and unfailing support!

Contents

Acknowledgments

We have many people who help us keep balanced on every level of our lives. All are friends and supporters who make our path easier and more pleasant to walk.

Our Teachers – with whom we could talk, ask questions, and who supported our souls while we walked the trail to a completed book.

Deb Herman

Judythe London

Cindy Van Rooy

Jacqueline Sussman

Veronica Willson

Sidney Haygood

Chrisida Almberg

Mary Bazley

Dr. Rosemarie Monaco

Sue Graves

Rev. Cecily Stranahan

Our Earth Angels: These dear people have all helped us with their own time and physical **WORK**!

Jeff Herman – Our agent, who knows a great book when he sees one.

Suzanne Mark – Secretary, Receptionist, Proof Reader, Jack of all Trades, and Daughter. It doesn't get any better than that.

Katie and *Caroline Griswold* – the best two daughters a mother could ever hope for. Thank you for your love and support.

Carrie Lewis-McGraw – the BEST of the BEST Publicists.

Dawn Thompson – you are the link between author and publication and the one who keeps track of the pieces and parts. This book could have never become possible without your help and we thank you.

Rita Johnson and *Ed Tyler* – Thank you for giving us a place to complete *Heaven & Beyond*.

We especially wish to acknowledge the angels and the deceased ones who came in droves to support us. We were always aware of their presence and encouragement.

Most of all, thanks to those who took the time to share their personal stories. By their courage, all of us have learned and grown.

Unfortunately we were unable to include all the wonderful stories we received. We hope that the account of your experience was a valuable part of your healing process and that you gained by sharing it with us. For those of you who sent stories that do not appear, please know we were honored to read them and they represent the seeds for our next book. May God and the angels bless you.

Barbara and Trudy

Life's Journey

Our journey through life reminds me of school
Moving one grade to the next
Seeing and learning and trying new things
Competing to outshine the rest

Some days are filled. Some days seem empty.
Some days we learn nothing at all.
It's a constant struggle between right and wrong
But we choose if we stand or we fall.

Enlightenment comes after chapters of life
Soon our time to leave her grows near.
So we pass our knowledge to the ones we love
And move on without guilt or fear.

So please don't mourn for loved ones passed
The angels are guiding their way
Instead be proud and then celebrate
Their heavenly graduation day.

—Jacqueline Sicard

The Beginning

How Heaven & Beyond
Came to Be

Your first book was from your experiences.
Your second book was from your knowing.
Your third book was from the people.
This book is from Us.

...the angels

We are sisters who were raised in a small town in Iowa. We were living rather ordinary lives, when suddenly everything became extraordinary.

In 1991, we were awakened three weeks apart out of a sound sleep by our angels and were taught to communicate with them in writing. From those moments on, our lives have been devoted to teaching others how to receive a written communication from their angels. We teach what the angels have taught us. They guide us as we write and carry out their divine directives. Their messages are a gift from God, to the angels, to us, and finally, to you.

In 1995, our first book, *Angelspeake: How to Talk with Your Angels*, was published. It was the first time our teachings had been put in written form. Our second book, *The*

Angelspeake Book of Prayer and Healing, showed readers how to work with the angels. Our third book, called *The Angelspeake Storybook*, recounts some of the hundreds of true stories of angel encounters experienced by people everywhere.

Looking back on our writing career, we now realize that as we finished each of our previous books, the angelic realm had already begun to work with us on the next book, although we didn't know it at the time. As we completed *The Angelspeake Book of Prayer and Healing*, we saw that the final stories and messages in the book were speaking about the joy of returning to God. We learned that returning to spirit wasn't so bad; it was living on earth that was the challenge. We began to understand that "transition," or going back to spirit, was just another process of life and was no more important or worse than birth. In fact, it was very much the same—just a birth in reverse!

During that time, Trudy's best friend, Chris, died knowing her angels were with her. Frank, Barbara's close friend, kept asking during their last visit, "When can I go? When can I go?" In both cases, their final days were not filled with fear, but with peace and anticipation of finally being freed of the burdens of life.

When the angels told us that our next book was to be about dying, we were rather amazed. They said, *"Your next book will be about the soul's transition process through 'death' and how it really is."*

The angels' words will be written in italics throughout the book.

We asked our angels, "What is the correct way to begin a book about a soul's transition? This is a new topic for us."

And the angels answered, "*With Life, of course, Children. For LIFE is the gift that God has given you that you are ready to give back through 'death.' Thus the 'transition.' This is a book from us for the living so they may better understand the importance of the transition that everyone will ultimately experience. Nothing as important as transition is ever accidental or haphazard. God, the angels, the dying, the living, and the passed away all gather to assure the success and beauty of a safe return to the spiritual plane.*

Most of us are brought up to think of death as an ending, a final event relative to this physical lifetime. *Heaven & Beyond* will teach you that there is no death, only a transition from the current physical life, as we know it. Transition only takes you to a new stage or form of life. Thus, when we speak of death in this book, we are always speaking of the transition experience. Not an ending or a final chapter, but a beginning."

Neither of us had much experience with death or the transition process. Our sister, Jackie, had the greatest involvement in our parents' deaths. Dad died quickly in his sleep. Mother had a terminal illness that took many months to complete. Since Jackie lived in their hometown, she was the primary caregiver. Jackie's experience was hands-on while ours took place from a distance. It was difficult for all of us sisters, no matter where we were, because we had no concept of what was really happening. All we knew was that our father had died and we were devastated because we didn't get to say goodbye. Later, with Mom, we were devastated because we didn't know how to say goodbye.

None of us had a strong sense of what to do while the soul was in the transition time. We each had different ways of coping with the process of losing a parent. With our father, there was no process because he died suddenly. Our grief began with the knowledge that Dad was dead. With our mother, whose death process took more than a year, it was a series of many goodbyes. How we dealt with her passing was deeply personal and was actually about learning to cope with a life-changing and frightening event.

We each did the best we could. Frequent visits to Iowa and daily phone calls were the way we could help both Mother and Jackie and still take care of our duties in Wyoming and Connecticut. We learned there is no right or wrong way to support each other and to care for ourselves in a time of doubt, confusion, and worry. We also learned that even though we coped in different ways, each of us could still have a memorable and loving involvement in saying goodbye and in loving our mother during her final days.

Those were the only intimate experiences we ever had with death, and we were very curious as to how we could write a book on a subject we didn't know much about. As usual, the angels guided us. They said,

"You will from today on begin to ask for experiences from those who have had loved ones die. There are many you already

know who have lost children, spouses, parents, friends, and pets. These stories will form the basis of your book. You will talk to many and will hear countless stories of comfort and learning — stories to help alleviate grieving for others."

At every class and seminar we taught, we would invite our students to share their experiences on dying. We asked them for write ups of actual encounters with family members and friends who had passed over, many of which are shared in this book. We were amazed at the amount of mail, e-mail, and phone calls we received. It seemed like everyone needed to share his or her experience. We expected that the stories would be depressing, and that we were creating a compendium of human experiences that would be sad and painful. Instead, we heard the most beautiful, intimate, inspiring, and uplifting stories imaginable.

Then the angels gave us instruction to help us put it all together and to complete our vision of *Heaven & Beyond*. They told us,

"You will write this book from four different perspectives: You will talk to caregivers and to those who have supported the death process. You will speak to those who are dying. Those who have died will also come forward with their comforting words, experiences, and teachings. Then, as you have taught in your classes, we will also communicate from our angelic point of view."

Our angels told us that we were to teach others that they could "call up" their deceased friends and relatives and also that they could communicate with them in writing.

We were astounded! For years, we had been teaching how to contact divine sources such as angels and spiritual guides, but to use those same techniques to contact our departed relatives had never occurred to us. When those who had passed over came to us from time to time with their messages, they had initiated the communication. Now we were being told we could call them for messages just as we had spoken with the angels. We didn't have to wait for friends and loved ones to initiate contact. We could invite them to come to us. We sat down and tried it ourselves. It worked!

Here is our first message from our father who died in 1971 and who was one of the early members of Alcoholics Anonymous. We wrote, "Dad, are you there?"

He replied, "Hello, Barbara and Trudy. Yes, it is Daddy. I am watching you work so industriously and am amazed at what beautiful women you have become.

"Now, let me tell you how I died. For a long time before I actually 'died' I was leaving my body at night. I had terrible headaches and I did not feel well when I was 'inside' my body. At night, I would roam and visit my mother and father, Uncle Dick, and my old buddies who were already 'dead.' One night, I just didn't come back. My physical body was wearing down and my work was done, so I just decided to stay with them. Your mother had some stuff to learn without me there, so it worked out fine. There was really nothing more for me to do.

"People say when someone dies unexpectedly, 'Oh, he was so young' or 'He was such a good man (or woman) and could have helped so many more.' But the truth is, dear daughters, if I had had more to do, I would have done it. It's like an empty box of cereal. You could say, 'Oh, it's all gone. If there was more, so many hungry people could be fed.' But the truth is, the cereal was all used up in this box. There was no more cereal available to feed anybody. The needy and hungry were just going to have to find another box to get fed from. My box was empty.

"So, you do not hear from me much. I am busy. As I helped people in life, I help them over here, too. There are many youngsters who take too many drugs and drink too much alcohol. I help them find a better life on earth. It was my favorite thing to do in life, and it is my favorite thing to do over here, too. There are more young drunks needing help than there are old drunks to help them some days. But it is working and God sends us what we need when we ask. Yes, even we have to 'ask,' too.

"Keep on doing what you are doing. You are reaching a lot of people. And more are coming to you every day to learn about how much God loves them. I love you, dear ladies. (I can't call you 'girls' anymore). Daddy"

As we began to compile the stories we received, the angels told us to put the book into five parts:

The Caregiver: which provides wisdom for families and friends as they help the person in transition.

The Dying One: which provides help for those preparing to pass over.

The Other Side: which discusses how to recognize your loved one's presence after transition.

The Connection: which will teach you how to communicate with your deceased loved ones.

The Angels' Viewpoint: which shows that life never ends.

As we worked on this book, we learned priceless information from the angels' instruction and from the stories received from others. We learned that encounters with those passing over as well as with those who have already passed over are gifts that are healing and transformative. We learned that when you sit with the dying, you are the one who will be healed. We learned that during this time love is the energy that sustains everyone.

We also learned that there is much more to do in helping people pass over than holding their hands and being physically present. We learned that preparation for transition could be pleasant and useful—both for the one passing and for those remaining. Family connections and history need not disappear with the dying. We learned many ways to record important information for future generations.

We also learned that it is peaceful on the other side, unlike any place we know here. We learned that when people pass over they become only love, totally love. And if they have left some work undone on this side, they may need to communicate with loved ones for healing and to complete unfinished business. That communication with us can take any number of forms.

Messages from loved ones on the other side are abundant. Many of the stories we received were accounts of parents, spouses, lovers, children, and friends who returned to say they were okay and to ask us not to mourn. They said they weren't dead! They said they were still with us!

The message of this book is not just about what happens when friends and loved ones pass over, but also about how to establish a relationship with them *after* death. In this, like in all other areas of our life, our angels are there to help, support, and guide us as we communicate with a loved one who has already made the transition.

All the stories in this book are true, and they show you that those who have passed away are accessible and awaiting the chance to talk with us. Part 4, The Connection, will teach you how. The Four Fundamentals—Ask, Believe, Let Go, and Say Thank You—will teach you to make contact in writing, not only with your spiritual helpers, guides, and angels, but also with deceased loved ones.

This book is a gift to you from those who have passed over or who dwell on the other side. Their life on this plane may be over, but their existence continues in a better, happier place where all is love, and where there is peace and joy beyond human understanding. Through this book, you will learn that there is no ending to life. You will find there is a heaven—and beyond.

AN ANGEL MESSAGE: Now is the time for this book. Many are making their transition. You will learn that the time of physical death is a choice made by the highest part of the soul along with the timing and permission of God. You will learn how lessons continue after physical death. You will learn to be aware of the presence of your loved ones. We will answer many questions. Life is good and so is death, for they are the same. You will see.

Part I

The Caregiver:
How to Help

We are with you during this time.
Never forget our wings surround you, too.
. . . the angels

No one dies alone. Whether there are human helpers giving comfort and aid or spiritual beings who gather to assist in the transition process, there is always support. On this side of life, the caregiver, usually a family member or members, plays a vital role in making sure that the mental and physical needs of the dying one are met. This is no easy task. It takes a commitment and a great deal of love to be with someone while they are taking their final journey.

A swift transition can be a terrible shock, accompanied by feelings of helplessness. A longer transition gives time for caregivers to show their love and to say goodbye. In these chapters of Part I, we are speaking mainly to those who assist the dying. We dedicate these pages to those who take over the day-to-day roles of nurse, cook, advisor, and friend. We hope to help you by supporting your efforts with ideas of things you can do that are important and helpful and by sharing the stories of others who have been in your situation. You are the ones who have to hold it all together. May you find the assistance you need in these pages.

One

Give Love

When people are dying and are totally surrendered to the process, they emanate a special grace. These people exist in an extraordinary state of consciousness and have much to teach us.

A minister friend named Charles was in an advanced stage of lung cancer and an extraordinary state of consciousness when we visited him recently. Charles had lunch with us and Barbara's daughter, Suzanne, who later commented that she felt an incredible electric energy coming from Charles. As she sat beside him at lunch, she noticed that his energy seemed to be "buzzing" into her leg and arm. When we told him, he said, "My body is just doing what it does, and I am watching my dying process as I would watch a movie on a screen." His serenity and nonattachment made us realize that we were in the presence of a truly exceptional man.

Such precious encounters are healing and transformative for those whom they touch. You can see the gift in the experience.

What do you say to someone who is dying? What do you say to their family? How do you act? How can you help? What can you do? Rather than do something wrong, we often do nothing at all, because we aren't sure what is appropriate

Our friend Donna D. called us shortly after her husband was diagnosed with terminal cancer. She was crying and needed our support, but during the conversation she said, "I don't know what to do. I've never done this before. I don't know how to act!" She wanted to be the best wife she could be during Ralph's final months, but her lack of experience in such a situation brought up all her insecurities and uncertainties. Most caregivers feel this way in the beginning.

There is only one rule in helping someone die—give love. If you give love by making delicious food, then cook. If you give love by singing, then sing. If you give love by reading, then read. If you give love by soothing, then soothe. If your presence is all you can give, then just *be* there. You don't have to say or do a thing. Everyone can make a contribution to the excellence of a passing. Give love if you can't give anything else.

Two

Listen and Talk

The transition process can bring up many fears, both in the caregiver and in the one dying. We have found this may not actually be the fear of death but rather about the pain and loneliness that accompany dying. Nurses tell us that if actual physical pain can be alleviated—or better still, eliminated—the dying process need not be unpleasant.

In some cases, especially with a long-term illness, by the time the actual death is imminent, the dying person has pretty much done everything that could be done and is ready to go. There may even be a type of eagerness to "get on with it." At that point, a gathering of friends and relatives can be a comfort, with a total loving focus on the one about to make the transition. The care receiver becomes the complete center of attention as every whim becomes important and is granted lovingly.

When Opal's brother was dying, the telephone proved to be a wonderful way for her to help him, counsel him, and love him during his final days. She told us, "My brother and I had so many good talks before he died. I told him I would call him every night and visit with him for five minutes. One night I told my brother a story about our mother's passing—about how Mother wanted to know what was going to happen. I told her she would see the light, that someone would be there to meet her, and that she would see her family. My brother was so glad that I shared that story with him.

"Another time we had the best talk about what he was going to find when he arrived at the other side. I told him about angels, and he said that was wonderful. We both knew he was going to die. He said, 'Dying isn't so bad. It's getting there that's so hard.'

"At the end, we became closer than we had ever been. Neither of us had been in good enough health to travel, and I had not seen him for ten years. It was the best time we ever had together. Talking through the death process really brought us together in life."

Sometimes the best way a caregiver can help is to allow or encourage the dying person to talk, talk, and talk—about whatever *they* want to talk about. The caregiver's job is simply to listen. Some people in transition need to talk about their experiences, whatever they may be. Our mother, Dorothy, couldn't talk enough about what was happening to her. She told us family stories we had never heard. She told us about our lives as children, and she told us how much she loved us. She talked about her feelings, her symptoms, and her fears. She talked about the things she wanted to give away, to whom, and how. She talked about her funeral, the songs she wanted sung, and the clothes she wanted to be buried in. She talked about her will. Our mother had never been so open and loving with us during her life. In truth, her last months of living were her finest and most loving days.

We sisters now feel that Mom had lived her whole life just to die as she did. Although it was horrible, it was also perfect and special for all of us. It was a wonderful time. She was more connected to life and to her family while dying than she ever had been.

While Trudy's friend Chris went to the hospital every few weeks for chemotherapy, it was a good time for the two friends to visit without phones, car pools, and general busyness of life getting in the way. They sat together for hours, enjoying each other's company. There were times when Chris wanted to talk about what was on her mind. She talked about her love and hopes for her husband and children. She talked about her love of God and His angels, as well as her friendship with Trudy. She shared the parts of her life that were important to her. It was a beautiful time of love that has become a treasured memory for Trudy, and it helped her prepare to say goodbye to her best friend.

Chris was as concerned about her family as they were about her. When she knew it was time to go, she asked her husband, daughter, and son if it was okay to let go. With her family at her bedside, Chris asked each one, "Is it alright if I leave now?" With hearts full of love, they said, "Yes, it's okay." With that, Chris closed her eyes and peacefully passed over.

Also, before people pass, they sometimes seem to come and go, as if no one is home within their bodies. In truth, the soul is leaving the body on short trips. Often during such times, the sick person gets confused as the illness deepens or medication clouds the mind.

Jerry's mother looked at him strangely one day and said, "Are you dead?" The question broke Jerry's heart, but his mother really just wanted to know which side of life she was on. Was she alive, or was she dead? Jerry was his mother's reality check!

Communicating with sick people isn't really hard. Just have normal conversations with those who want to talk. Follow their lead while you converse. Ask them questions, enjoy their stories, and listen, listen, listen.

Three

Respect Privacy

For others, talking is *not* desired. Respect the privacy of those you care about and follow their lead, whether you like it or not.

Caregivers working with dying people are in an awkward position. Many have not had any experience with death. They may have their own fears, and they may be grieving for the dying person. The caregiver's own physical and financial resources may be completely stressed, and there may also be family pressures on the caregiver.

Whatever the situation, the caregiver should focus on doing what is best for the *care receiver*. Ask the person and family what they need, would like to have, want, or would like you to do, and follow their direction, even if it doesn't meet *your* needs.

In the 1960s, Barbara had four friends with whom she played cards every Thursday afternoon. One of the friends, called Jane, was diagnosed with cancer during her fourth pregnancy. The women's concern and their desire to help Jane was overwhelming. However, Jane and her husband decided they wanted to deal with the problem alone. He told the other women that nothing was to be said about her illness. If the word *cancer* was even mentioned, they would not be playing cards with her again.

From then on, every Thursday, the four ladies got together to play cards, but they never said a syllable about what was going on. To everyone's joy, Jane's baby was born healthy. As her disease progressed, Jane carried chemo bags with her each Thursday, but again, nothing was ever said. She lost weight, and still there was no discussion about her illness. It was an agonizing year for everyone that continued until Jane's death. However, Jane's friends respected her wishes. If she had wanted to talk about her illness, she had plenty of opportunity every week. Yet she never did. It may not have been Jane's friends' way to cope with illness, but it was Jane's. The other women did not intrude because they loved her and respected her privacy.

Sometimes we get caught up in guilt because we don't feel we did everything we could have done. We may also feel that if our loved one passes over, it means we've done something wrong. "Did I say the right prayers? Did I pray too much . . . not enough . . . not hard enough . . . not long enough?" Trust that you did the best you could. God's plan is always in action. You did the best you could, and it was perfect.

Four

Family and Friends

There are as many ways to care for someone who is dying as there are people. Some people take the inevitable as a natural process of life. Others fight it to the last breath. This chapter includes stories that others have shared with us about how people supported each other as they were passing over.

Marilyn cherishes the memory of her father-in-law's passing. She writes, "During the time my father-in-law had cancer, my husband and I visited him every month or so. We felt that we really needed to be there for him. Near the end, other family members took him out to his farm to see it for one last time. The next day he was very slow and didn't seem to recognize some of us. Not knowing how long he would live, we called in the rest of the family, and when everyone was there the whole family said goodbye.

"For a minute, my sister-in-law and I were alone with Dad in the room. We told him that the angels were there and that it was okay to go if he saw his angels. 'We know you will be fine,' we said. As the rest of the family came back into his room, he let go. It was so peaceful! I had been afraid of what would happen during his last minutes of life, but it was just peaceful. Everything worked out just right and it was beautiful. It was a good death."

Marion shares a similar story about the passing of her husband, Don. She explains, "Don approached the hour of his death with the same qualities with which he lived his life. He had suffered from cancer, which had consumed his physical abilities, but not his compassion for us. Don was a scientist, a Ph.D. physicist, and a teacher, and he was gifted with a great combination of humor and intellect. He wanted us to understand what was happening to him.

"His story begins early on a Sunday morning. All the family was at the hospital. Our family is so small that we could hold his hands and touch the man we loved as his life was ebbing away. He spoke to us, saying, 'Listen, listen, can you hear me?' There were tears in his eyes as he said, 'I'm dying. I'm so tired. I'll try . . . I'll be back. I'll tell you.' Then he described what he saw, and said, 'A lot of people, so many people. 1 . . . 2 . . . 3 . . . 4 . . . 5 . . . 6 . . . 7 . . . 8 . . . 9 . . . 10 . . . 11 . . . 12. There are 12 of them, you know. The Gentleman is here. I saw Dad. He says he loves me. Don't worry about me. I'm finished. Oh my goodness, goodness. . . I don't know. We'll see.'

"When his breath was gone, and his body changed so quickly, we were able to recognize the magnificent gift that had just been bestowed on all of us in his family. The gift of knowing, the certainty of knowing that our Heavenly Father had welcomed Don. Our Lord gathered him in and made Himself known to us at 9 A.M. on Sunday morning, June 20, Father's Day."

Lingering illnesses give friends or loved ones the opportunity to rally behind and support the sick person and each other. Here is Theresa's story about how the tables were turned and she was healed. She begins, "After my mom and dad died, I vowed not to get involved with people who were old or ill. It hurt too much when they died! But things change!

"My next-door neighbor is a wonderful woman whom we call Honey Mom. She helps many in our community and is everything I hope to become some day. Honey Mom became sick and was unable to continue visiting a little old lady named Bessie, who had Alzheimer's. She asked if we would visit Bessie in her place while she was ill. (It was the best thing that could have happened to us!) My daughter and I went to the nursing home to visit Bessie on a daily basis, and we really enjoyed our visits even though she didn't always recognize us.

"Bessie came down with pneumonia and was put in the hospital, where we visited her two or three times a day. A stroke followed, and her anger and frustration were clearly visible. The Bessie of yesterday was gone, but I put my feelings aside because I knew she really needed me. I was with her on her last day on earth. I held her hand and told her how much she was loved. I will miss Bessie! She gave me more than I ever gave her!"

Disease debilitates all parts of the body, mind, and spirit. Nothing escapes its onslaught. Sweet, loving Bessie became angry and mean. Theresa found patience to deal with the changes in Bessie, but not everyone can. Remember that when your friend or loved one's personality becomes unlovable, it is not the person who is speaking or behaving badly; it is the disease. The disease is angry and mean. Not the person.

It can be easy to burn out when you're acting as a caregiver. Friends or relatives who must support a sick person day in and day out—and not miss any steps or drop any balls along the way—can be overwhelmed with relentless demands. In such an environment, caregivers can become emotionally aloof and machine-like, jumping from crisis to crisis, denying their own emotional pain.

Here are three things to look for if you think you may be burning out. If you can relate to even one of these, get some help for yourself! You cannot help others if you don't help yourself first.

1. Detachment (especially from the dying person)
2. Exhaustion (both physical and emotional)
3. Loss of satisfaction or sense of accomplishment

Use the word HALT to check your levels of stress. If you are having difficulty coping, ask yourself if you are too *Hungry, Angry, Lonely,* or *Tired.* This is an easy self-check to know when to ask for help. Becoming a martyr serves no one. You do not have to feel as bad as the person who is dying to show that you care. Be good to yourself! As a caregiver, seek your own support system and ask your own friends for help. Caregivers also need care. Above all, know your limitations.

Everyone experiences grief in their own way, but often there are recognized stages to the grief process. It starts at the recognition of a loss and extends to the eventual acceptance of it. Usually the stages of grief include shock, denial, anger, bargaining, depression, and finally acceptance. Responses will vary depending upon the circumstances associated with the death. It helps to know the stages of grief and what they are so you can see yourself go through them. The one you are caring for will also go through these stages, for there is a grief process within the dying process. It helps to be more tolerant of everyone when you know what happens.

Grief is an essential response to loss that should not be prevented. Refusing to deal with the loss of a loved one, or being unable to face the loss, may cause an absent or delayed grief reaction. Grief not expressed openly might come out in other ways, such as physical symptoms, depression, or erratic behavior, or possibly feelings displaced onto other persons.

When someone we know or love is ill or dies, we want that person to be with us still. We desire their presence and companionship. We long for the connection we once had, or possibly the desire to say one last thing. We can be overwhelmed by waves of wishes that will never be met. No matter what the circumstances of the death, grief is a necessary process for healing the loss of a loved one.

Five

Hospice Care

Help from a hospice can seem like a gift from the heavens during final days. Hospice is a program or facility that provides a care-giving team of professionals to help terminally ill patients and their families. Many dying people would prefer to spend their last days at home, alert and free of pain, among the people and things they love. Hospice care makes that possible. Your physician will tell you when the time is right to call a hospice. Also your doctor will have a list of facilities in your area.

Even more important, hospice care can be a family's salvation. By the time the final days commence, the entire family may be exhausted. The best can be brought out in a family during a death crisis, but unfortunately, so can the worst. It starts to feel as though everyone's personality is magnified, and fear overwhelms or anger erupts instantaneously.

Quick deaths are shocking in their suddenness, but when a person has been lingering for months and months, the physical, mental, spiritual, and financial resources of a family may be totally depleted. Hospice help can be given in the home and enables families to remain together in peace, comfort, and dignity.

Most family members say, "I do not know what I would have done without hospice care." As Beverly G. explains, "My step-dad of 33 years is about to make his transition. The hospice team has been calling on him for several weeks. Recently, his condition worsened, and they have started to come each day. If Dad is having an especially bad day, Janice, his hospice volunteer, makes an extra trip to see him. Janice also gave me her telephone number so I could call her to ask her any questions. She really cares for him and has taken a personal interest in him. His wife is very small and can't lift him, so the hospice team sends a person to help her two hours a day. That means she can get out of the house or get to the market.

"Hospice care has been invaluable to us. If it weren't for the hospice team, he wouldn't be able to stay at home where he is comfortable. Dad told his wife that he is looking for his dad, who passed over 20 years ago. He said that when he finds Grandpa, it will be time for him to go, and for his sake I hope he can go soon."

Often a home setting isn't appropriate for the last days. Many hospice groups can move the dying person to a total care facility, where family and friends can be supported by a staff especially trained in helping everyone through the transition process. All-in-all, hospice facilities get an A+! They provide families with specific support during the transition process, allow them to come and go as needed, and help them learn not to be afraid.

Judy G.'s family remains thankful for the care their beloved aunt received through a hospice program. She reflects, "One of the things that comforted me most when my Aunt Ganka died was the treatment we received in the hospice facility. The entire experience was very moving.

"When we went in, I saw that the front door had a huge carving of the Tree of Life on it, and the symbolism was remarkable. Everyone had warm and sincere smiles on their faces, and we felt welcome and safe. I was having a difficult time with her passing, and the staff was as attentive to me as they were to her. I slept there part of the first night, and I was grateful when a nurse came in and sat down with me. She comforted me and helped me with my grief.

"Families were allowed to come in and out any time they wanted to. I was even able to bring in my aunt's dog for a final goodbye. Love abounded there, and one can rest assured that the final moment of someone's life will be treated with respect and dignity.

"God bless the workers in hospice care. They have incredibly kind hearts, and they truly knew how to help my aunt pass over into the light."

Six

Medical Facilities

Many people transition in a hospital setting. We have received many letters about the care experienced by loved ones in medical facilities. Some people complain about the lack of support caregivers and patients receive in a hospital or nursing home. But others have wonderful stories to share. During her father's passing, Judythe was supported and helped by caring nurses and a remarkable doctor, in an excellent hospital. She notes, "I waved goodbye to my 85-year-old father as they closed the ambulance doors, telling him I would meet him at the hospital. I called my angels as I started the car and drove through the familiar streets, suddenly overcome with the thought that he could be dying. The feeling I must hurry became more urgent.

"I parked the car under the emergency room sign, grabbed the Power of Attorney file, and ran through the entrance to the admitting desk. My heart was pounding as I told the clerk who I was and that it was my father's wish not to be resuscitated. The clerk hurried down the hall and returned immediately with a tall, dark-eyed doctor. He asked if I had Power of Attorney for Healthcare, and I handed the documents to him. I had learned from my mother's death six months earlier that if hospitals can't find the "no resuscitate" orders that they have on file, hospital policy requires them to resuscitate.

"The doctor said, 'Come with me.' There was only one other patient in the emergency room, and I knew that would give Daddy a better chance to have the complete attention of the staff. But I didn't know that the doctor would act as a guardian angel to my father and me throughout the next hour.

"Daddy was propped up on a gurney and was still alert. I was relieved to see they had not yet attached him to any life support equipment. The doctor put his arm around my shoulder and guided me to Daddy's bedside. 'Your daughter tells me that you have stated that you do not wish to be resuscitated and that she has Power of Attorney. Is that true?'

"Daddy's eyes found mine. This moment was as holy as any moment I have ever experienced. 'Yes, that's right,' Daddy said, and closed his eyes. He had made his choice to let go.

"The doctor asked if anyone else was coming. I told him my sister and son were on their way. The doctor seemed to read my mind. 'You don't have to leave him. Stand right here beside him,' he told me. My heart leapt. Then it hit me. Daddy, his strong muscled body, unlined face, looking years younger than his 85, was dying. I had never seen anyone die before. 'How long?' I could barely mouth the words.

"'I can't say. Just stay by him,' he whispered.

"The rest of my family arrived and I was overwhelmed with the feeling that in some way I should help my father with his crossing. I prayed silently that all those who were ready to receive my father on the other side of this life would start the party. I prayed that I would know what to do to help the process. I instinctively reached out my hands and put them on his chest. I could feel the faint but steady beat of Daddy's dear heart. I could feel my eyes jumping behind my closed lids. In my completely relaxed state I could 'see' his welcoming committee awaiting his transition. I was 'in' Daddy's death experience!

"I felt Daddy's energy move into space. It was as though he was slowly testing his new state without gravity while still connected to his body. I felt my hands on his heart were somehow grounding his body so he could experiment with his newfound freedom.

"Suddenly I felt a big WHOOSH! and he took off. I felt his soul go from his body, through my hands, and on to God. He had been transported just like on *Star Trek*. Dad loved *Star Trek* and now he was getting to do it.

"I opened my eyes, and when I looked at Daddy's face I was shocked to see that the essence of who he had been had disappeared. There before me lay only a body so completely void of Daddy I couldn't believe it was him. The soul illuminates the body in such a way that without the soul we are nothing.

"Daddy took leave of this life with great grace and dignity, and he gave me the gift of trusting me to go part way with him. I was given the privilege of noninterference and full support of a hospital staff who said they wished all deaths could be like Daddy's, who died the captain of his own departure."

Cindy had a different experience when her father died. "I wouldn't have known he was dead if I hadn't been looking at the monitor. He was there, and then he wasn't. He just slipped away."

In another positive story, Wayne's daughter Pat shares her experience of his last day. She explains, "We had been at the hospital night and day for 21 days, and we were exhausted.

Thank God for the wonderful staff at the hospital. They helped us all get through Dad's dying.

"I will always remember Dad's last day. We walked in as the nurses had just finished washing his head. He had been in a coma or semi-coma for about five days. He hadn't talked or opened his eyes—nothing. Up to that time, he didn't recognize people. He thought I was his sister, Dorothy."

Vera, Wayne's wife, adds, "When we were on our way up to Wayne's room we heard laughter coming out of it. I looked at Pat and said, 'Dad must be feeling better.' I asked everyone in his room, 'What was so funny?' They told me he had been telling his stories.

"I stood there a second or two and he said, 'Come over here; I want to give you a kiss.' So I went around the bed, and I kissed him. The nurses were continuing his bath, so I said we would leave for about 20 minutes. When we returned, Wayne was no longer conscious. I feel we were blessed by sharing his last lucid moments and that he recognized us before passing over."

Pat continues, "He passed away that night. I didn't think I wanted to go to the hospital after he died, but I am so happy I did. He looked so tranquil, and quiet, and peaceful. That is what I remember most after my Dad passed away."

Vera agrees, "I can't get over that beautiful look he had on his face. He was so content."

If your hospital or nursing facility has not lived up to your expectations, ask to speak to the Director of Nursing, the Chief Administrator, the social worker on staff, or the patient advocate. One of them will be able to help you.

Seven

Remember Me

Caregivers can play a vital role long before the person is ready to cross to another realm. There may be months of pleasant and useful preparation. During this time, the caregiver and care receiver can spend many enjoyable hours creating a legacy for children and grandchildren that will live on for generations.

Too often in our society the family tree is incomplete. Few can name all eight of their great-grandparents by name. Yet great-grandparents are just three generations away, only about 60 years. Future generations will thank you for taking the time to fill in the baby books, family bibles, and family genealogical trees with all the ancestors you can identify. Often only the oldest family members can supply names, birth dates, marriages, children, and other pertinent information. This is a great time to gather that information.

In addition, you could also include little anecdotes or vignettes about the people. What jobs did the grandparents hold? Did they have any hobbies, successes, diseases, or talents? Even just a few words could be a great help to others fascinated with family genealogy.

Organizing a Lifetime

People usually love to talk about their past. A few pointed or directed questions now will be helpful when family members want answers years later.

It isn't uncommon for people to change their names, move, or call loved ones by nicknames or family endearments, and then the family history is lost to future generations. To prevent this from happening, follow this checklist to get as much pertinent information as you can before a person makes the transition.

Full name and correct spelling (this should match the
  birth certificate)
Birth date, time, and location
What was happening in the world at that time
Facts about parents
Memories about grandparents
Information about brothers and sisters
The earliest memory
Family legends
Personal history (stories can include ages 1–5;
  elementary school; middle school; high school;
  and any other education)
Things the person would have liked to do
Things the person is glad to have done
Things the person would change
Wars during the lifetime
What people wore over the years (hats, gloves, shoes,
  fabrics, etc.)

Strongest memories (good and bad)
Favorites (books, movies, clothes, etc.)
Friends
Favorite foods
Routines
Hobbies (sports, crafts, etc.)
Awards

Web Sites and E-mail

Family Web sites are quite easy to set up and provide a great way for the ill person to keep in touch with those who cannot come to visit. Start taking pictures early to put on a Web site. Add progress reports and cheerful notes to help everyone keep in touch. Remember, electronic mail and Web sites can function both ways. Friends and relatives can e-mail pictures, greetings, and news to the ill person as well.

Our friend Donna K. made up a site when her sister was killed in a bicycle accident. Whether family or friends could attend the services or not, it was possible for everyone to participate in the family gathering that was taking place online. Donna added lots of pictures and invited others to contribute memories about her sister's life. It was a wonderful way for an extended family to stay together during a very difficult time.

Writing a Life Journal

When Julie became pregnant, she had an urge to tell her unborn baby about all that she had done in her life. Julie began to write about her feelings, her daily life experiences, and her hopes and aspirations for her child's future. After Casey was born, Julie continued to write, and over the years the journal grew in size and scope.

As Casey began school, Julie discovered that she had advanced cancer. She didn't know what the outcome would be, but she wanted her daughter to know what was in her heart and mind for her child. She wrote daily until she was too ill to hold the pen to paper.

Julie not only gave Casey life, she gave her continuous, daily evidence of her unconditional love. She left a written heritage that will be treasured forever by Casey. Julie's greatest wish was that her daughter would never forget her mother and her love for her. This journal ensures that Casey never will forget.

Videos and Audio Recordings

Ill or elderly people often don't have the strength to write. Friends and family members can encourage them to reminisce verbally about the "olden days." If you have the technology available, help your loved ones tell their story through audio recordings and videos. Ask them to tell stories about their past, their family, and their life experiences. Use the interview technique to aid their memory. Or you could do what Donna K.'s family did, by assembling all the memorabilia of her father's lifetime to put on videotape.

One day on television, we saw a woman who was in chemotherapy and wasn't sure what her prognosis would be. She had made a very extensive video for her daughter including all of the things she had hoped to teach the child in person. The videotape included how to put on makeup and perfume, how to make favorite family recipes, how to behave on a date, and so forth. This loving legacy helped give the mother closure and the daughter a lasting life-map of her mother's values, gifts, and talents.

Memorials

Dorothy's son, Bob, and his wife both died of cancer two years apart, leaving a three-year-old daughter. Friends and supporters who wanted to help began a leukemia fund in Illinois, where the family was living. Many people in Illinois now wear a "Blue Angel" pin to show their support for leukemia research, and to remind others that angels are on earth as well as in heaven.

Memory Quilt

Friends made a "Get Well" quilt for Laurile. Each friend made a quilt square depicting a part of Laurile's personality that they liked best or hobbies they knew she enjoyed. While she was gravely ill, she was encouraged and comforted by wrapping herself in the love it represented. Today she is back at work with the very people who made the quilt and prayed for her so effectively. Her recovery shows that prayer works, and her quilt will forever remind Laurile of her friends' love and prayers for her.

Eight

Paperwork

When our father died, our mother couldn't find an important paper. We looked everywhere for it. Finally, we looked in a safe deposit box that Mom and Dad had kept for years, but since we didn't have the key, we had to get bank officers and an attorney to authorize its opening. It was an unnecessary hassle when it would have been so much easier if Dad had just told Mother where the safe deposit key was.

If you are legally entitled to do so, gather together the following items: bank accounts, passbooks, certificates of deposit, money market funds, stocks, bonds, precious metals, jewelry, real estate deeds, promissory notes, contracts, insurance policies, safety deposit boxes (including location of the key), and retirement or pension benefits.

Other important documents, such as birth and marriage certificates, social security numbers, military service records, divorce decrees, property settlements, income tax returns (both state and federal), death certificate of spouse (if any), and wills (including the attorney's name and executor) or trust agreements, should be listed and the locations designated. If able, the dying person should complete the list. If that's not possible, a family member, attorney, banker, accountant, or certified financial planner can help compile the inventory, which should then be copied and kept in a safe, obvious place, possibly with a relative or friend. It is important that these documents be updated every year . . . preferably long before death is imminent. These records should be readily available to all family members.

Remember, as a caregiver concerned about the financial affairs of a care receiver, don't get directly involved without legal authority. Acting without clear legal authority, even with the best of intentions, can cause serious problems.

A Durable Power of Attorney is a written legal document giving someone other than the principal or owner the authority to make financial decisions. The principal must sign this while he or she is still legally competent.

A Durable Power of Attorney for Health Care authorizes someone other than the sick or dying person to make medical and health care decisions on his or her behalf. It allows people to specify ahead of time how they wish these decisions to be made. Decisions regarding extraordinary supportive care, including breathing machines and tube feeding, can be addressed in this document. All adults should have a Durable Power of Attorney for Health Care.

Nine

Organ Donation

Your loved ones can live on for years if they are able to help someone else through organ donation. Kathleen and Bruce called the coroner within minutes after learning that their 21-year-old son, Nathaniel, had been killed in a car accident. Because it was the middle of the night, they couldn't reach the proper people to donate their son's organs. They knew that time was of the essence, so they persisted in their search until they found Shawn, whose life work is to find organ donors. Because of their persistence in a time of enormous grief, more than 75 people were helped as a result of their son's death.

Here is the actual letter they received from the Inland Eye and Tissuebank:

On behalf of the Inland Eye and Tissuebank I want to extend my deepest sympathies to you on the death of your son. Even though it has been 2½ years since he was taken from you, I know that there is probably not a day that goes by that you don't miss him. I did want to let you know that he touched many lives through the donation of his tissues.

We recovered Nate's eye tissue so that we could use his sclera to help glaucoma patients. Eight people were helped, which includes a 3-year-old boy in San Bernardino, a 22-year-old woman in Loma Linda, a 22-year-old woman in Riverside, a 33-year-old woman in Rialto, a 51-year-old woman in Riverside, a 68-year-old man in Big Bear, a 71-year-old woman in Redlands, and a 72-year-old man in Riverside.

When we recovered Nate's heart tissue, we were gratified to see that both valves would help give life to two people who were suffering from heart disease. Nate's pulmonary valve was implanted on May 6 into a 40-year-old man living in Canada. His aortic valve was implanted on August 5 into a 74-year-old man living in Sacramento.

Even though we do not know the specific recipients and their medical problems, we do know that Nate's bone and cartilage tissues may have helped as many as fifty people who had suffered traumatic injuries, degenerative disease, or cancerous tumors. The gift of mobility and freedom from pain is truly a blessing.

On behalf of the many lives that have been transformed through one young man that will never be forgotten, please accept my profound gratitude.

Time is critical in organ donation. Find out all the information you can before your loved one passes. There are different rules for "harvesting" different organs. The circumstances surrounding a death largely determine what can be donated. Major organs, such as heart, lungs, kidneys, and others, must be harvested under special conditions in a hospital. Eyes, bones, skin, and other less delicate parts are more easily given. Most hospitals have a staff member you can contact for further information. Do not assume, just because an individual is identified as an organ donor on a driver's license, that the organs will be donated automatically.

In a *Dear Abby* column about organ donation, she pointed out that 66,717 people were on organ donor waiting lists and 4,800 people had died waiting to receive a donated organ. The following philosophy by Robert Test gave us a clear perspective that we'd like to share with you.

To Remember Me - by Robert Test

At a certain moment, a doctor will determine that my brain has ceased to function and that, for all intents and purposes, my life has stopped. When that happens, do not attempt to instill artificial life into my body by the use of a machine. And don't call this my "deathbed." Call it my "bed of life," and let my body be taken from it to help others lead fuller lives.

Give my sight to a man who has never seen a sunrise, a baby's face, or love in the eyes of a woman. Give my heart to a person whose own heart has caused nothing but endless days of pain. Give my blood to the teenager who has been pulled from the wreckage of his car, so that he might live to see his grandchildren.

Give my kidneys to one who depends on a machine to exist from week to week. Take my bones, every muscle, every fiber and nerve in my body, and find a way to make a crippled child walk. Explore every corner of my brain. Take my cells, if necessary, and let them grow so that some-day a speechless boy will shout at the crack of a bat and a deaf girl will hear the sound of rain against her windows.

Burn what is left of me and scatter the ashes to the winds to help the flowers grow. If you must bury something, let it be my faults, my weaknesses and all my prejudice against my fellow man.

Give my sins to the devil. Give my soul to God. If, by chance, you wish to remember me, do it with a kind deed or word to someone who needs you. If you do all I have asked, I will live forever.

As a family member, you will have to pursue your loved one's wishes. Organ donation decisions need to be discussed before death, not after, so you can do what they desire.

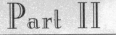 Part II

The Dying One:
Preparing to Pass Over

This is a time of birth back home.
This is a time of joy for the soul.
. . . the angels

There really is *no* death. Dying is a release of earth life that returns our soul to the dimension from which we originally came. We will recognize friends, family members, souls, spiritual guides, and angels we left behind when we were born. Everything will seem familiar, and we will be enormously glad to have made this final trip. *Rejoicing* is the key word for this time. It is a grand homecoming.

Transition is the final spiritual event of our physical life on earth. Although we will all make this journey, myths, fears, and old beliefs can prevent us from receiving the help available from our angels and friends on the other side.

Death is never an accident. The timing may surprise us, but there is a larger plan at work for all of us, whether we understand it or not. There are many levels of life beyond our knowing.

Our angels explained it to us this way.

Dear Children,

Please don't make transition so hard. Let's talk about this thing called "death." When you have a birthday, do you consider that you have "died"? Do you say, "I am no longer 20, so I have died and therefore gone into new dimensions and understandings"? No, of course not. Do you think you have "died" when you move from one house to another? Do you think you have "died" when you marry because you left the single state? Do you think you have "died" when you leave one job and take on another? Of course you don't. It would be against common sense to think these things. You are merely growing from one phase or experience to the next. One life experience only leads you to another and another as your soul learns lessons and you move forward. And so it is when you transition from life to afterlife.

Obviously, those living their final days on earth are the ones most vitally interested in transition. Some of these people are terrified; others experience great peace, calmness, and acceptance. No matter what the emotional state of the dying person, the process certainly dwarfs in importance any other experience in his or her life. Often the dying person is the least afraid, and will attempt to comfort others. Fear of the unknown is often greater with family members than within the person in transition.

There are many ways to approach the transition of your soul. How your family and close friends treated the death process when you were young will affect your attitudes about dying and transition later in life. Families with a sound understanding of life, death, and spirituality are usually honest and open in discussing their feelings. Others become extremely fearful and attempt to avoid as much as possible even the mention of the death process.

Just as families are different, so are members within a family, who may each have their own attitudes and methods of dealing with the inevitable event that all of us face. Some act as if death is not inevitable—as if by refusing to recognize its reality they won't experience it.

In this part of *Heaven & Beyond*, we relate stories of those who were unafraid to return to spirit, and those who were burdened with fear as they returned to spirit. We can learn how to reduce the fear of dying through the experiences of others.

Ten

Childhood Experiences

Sometimes, childhood experiences create myths and misunderstandings that need to be healed later. Well-meaning adults who are not well informed can create a lifelong fear of death in the hearts of children who have not had a chance to develop a mature understanding of the reality and certainty of death. You can easily imagine the fear of death that was established in a young child's life as a result of the following true stories.

Virginia explains, "I had so many fears about death when I was young. I was told that they only showed the top part of a person in the coffin because they cut off the bottom part. I don't remember who told me that, but I sure believed it. When I went to church, I had to pass a vacant lot next to the funeral home, and that's where I thought they buried the bottom part."

Mel also developed a fearful view of death. She notes, "As a child, I believed that the person who had died was put in a position of watchfulness and authority over me. I believed they were God-like and they could (and would) punish me for things that I did wrong. This affected my belief about dying because then I felt powerless and I wished I could be dead so I could punish those who I believed had hurt me. At the same time it made me even more fearful of dying, since I wasn't sure if I could be punished as well by other dead people after I died.

"I also believed angels had the power to punish me. This didn't even begin to change for me until I began serious and thoughtful communications with my own angels. Thank God my angels helped me to learn differently."

As a young girl, Grace developed a fear of death that has stayed with her to this day. She notes, "When I was a child, the Sisters of Notre Dame taught me. At the time, the method of teaching children was to scare them to death. We were taught that if we did one thing wrong, we would go to hell when we died, or at least purgatory."

Grace shivers. "I could see myself in hell shoveling coal for all eternity."

She concludes, "I was a good child, but very impressionable. My childhood fear is still there, and thoughts of death still make me nervous."

Like Grace, Yvonne's mother picked up her fear from an adult. Yvonne explains, "When my mother was a very small child, she attended a funeral at a Catholic church. Not being Catholic, she had never seen incense, so she asked her dad what the smoke was all about. He replied, 'They're smokin' the devil out of him.' She said she believed that for a very long time!"

Laurie told us that she has suffered for years because her parents refused to recognize and accept death as a part of life. She says, "There is a large section of my life that has not been opened because my parents never mentioned death. One of my first memories concerned one of those little turtles that kids used to buy. I bought one and kept it in a bowl. One day it died, and my father came home and just threw it in the trash. I'll never forget that. I cried and cried. Later, when I was an adult, I asked my dad if he had a will. He just ignored me and said, 'Oh just throw me away when I go.'

"My parents would not tell me when a family member had died. I would miss someone and would ask about him or her and they said, 'Oh, he died three months ago.' One day, my mother came home and said, with no emotion, that her mother had died. I had another shock when my brother died. He was only 13 months older than I was. My mother showed absolutely no emotion.

"When my father died, my mother called me at work and said, 'I think your father is dead.' I drove to the house but I couldn't even look at him, and I didn't know what to do. Finally, I called the police and they took him away. I didn't go to his funeral. That's when I began to go to therapy. I have bought scores of books on death and have gone to four or five groups on death.

"I am terrified of dying, and I have been left in a terrible place. This has been very devastating to me. I'm 67 now, and although that's not 90, I think that if I was 87 or so, I should be afraid to die. When you get to my age, people around you die and you can't avoid it. I still don't go to funerals and haven't for years. I keep working on saying to myself, 'Well, you know you are going to die,' and then I say, 'God, it's awful.' That's my next step. I need to get over this hump."

Laurie assured us that her parents were good people. They were afraid of death, and this was their way of coping with their fear and grief. But what happened to the child Laurie has had lifelong repercussions for her.

Heaven only knows how many myths and misunderstandings we still harbor as adults that affect our attitudes toward death. If you find you are haunted with fear concerning this important life event, find a group or therapist who can help you work through your issues. We also hope *Heaven & Beyond* will show you that there is no reason to be afraid of transition.

Eleven

To Stay or to Go

Our angels will help us when our souls face a choice of life or death. On a conscious level, we do not know when our lessons are over and our work on earth is finished. Sometimes we think life is complete. Usually we are the last to know what is going on. Joe's father thought his life was complete and he was ready to die. In actuality, he still had more life to live, but when the timing was right, he did go.

Joe notes, "My father was furious when he didn't die! Dad was a feisty Italian who was used to making his own decisions. He didn't want to be alive anymore, was ready to die, and felt he would have been better off in the hands of his creator. It was his time to go.

"Dad had been ill with leukemia for many years and at various times went to the hospital for transfusions. Each time, he signed a paper saying he did NOT wish to be resuscitated if he expired.

"For some reason, when he went into the hospital just before Christmas, the paper didn't get signed. This time, he did pass on, and the Do Not Resuscitate order wasn't in effect. The hospital had to follow the laws of the State of New Jersey and resuscitate him.

"When my father could talk, he was angry—so angry that he spent two or three days complaining about being resuscitated. He kept saying, 'Make sure that damn paper is signed!' From then on, whenever he went to the hospital, that was the first thing he asked to do. Dad lived another six months. During that period, I got to spend a lot of time with him, and he met my future wife, which was very important for both of them. When he did go, he went peacefully, knowing that his wishes were being carried out."

Frank tells a similar story about his Uncle John. "My uncle was under the care of a physician who was helping him deal with depression over the loss of his sight. Uncle John had stopped eating, and by the time we went to see him in the hospital, he was very weak and barely able to speak. It was clear that he wanted the hospital staff to stop working on him so he could be allowed to die in peace. The family was concerned about Uncle John's failing health and wanted to do everything to keep him alive, but it was clear that my uncle was ready and wanted to die. We tried to convince the family that extraordinary means to keep him alive were not his wish. While it was difficult for the family to accept his wishes, they began to understand. Uncle John asked to be transferred back to the nursing home where his wife, Emma, was living so he could be with Emma to say goodbye.

"A few days later he passed away. After his death, the family began to understand that this was best for him and Emma, and we know he is in a better place. We will miss Uncle John, a strong but gentle man, who thought of others most of his life."

Remember that we always have free will. Our angels have told us that sometimes we are at a stopping place in our lives where we can choose to do more work, or we can choose to return to spirit. We are told that at these times we have completed segments of our learning and our soul has options for the future. Everything is part of a larger plan, but these options may come to us.

Lisa's angels came to her and gave her options to stay or go, and she has not regretted her decision to stay, in spite of the fact that it was the more difficult path.

She remembers, "I hadn't been sleeping because I was in a lot of pain. Three days before I went to the doctor to find out what was wrong with me, I felt my dead grandfather's presence around me. It was so soothing. I can't describe how it felt. One night, Grandpa came to me surrounded by angels. He said they had come to take me to heaven. The angels said that it was my choice, and I said, 'Yes! Yes!' almost immediately.

"The angels and Grandpa told me it would be peaceful and painless and that I would be going to a wonderful place. Grandpa held my hand and I felt like we were going—that we were on our way to heaven! Then I said, 'Wait, wait! I am not ready. I am not sure.' They told me it would be very hard if I stayed, but they would be with me the whole time. A lady angel said staying here would enrich my life and reassured me that the angels would help me. I remember being sad because I wanted to go with my Grandpa, but when I thought about leaving my earth family, I just couldn't do it. I am glad I made the decision to stay, but it was hard, just as they had said!

"My diagnosis was Non-Hodgkin's Lymphoma. Five days later I started the chemotherapy and the prognosis was very bad. I remember the angels coming into the room and staying with me at night. I never again felt like I was going to die. I wasn't afraid.

"The angels operated in every area of my life. Sometimes I felt so grateful that I was able to go through the cancer and everything that was related. It made me a different person. Regardless of how long I stay on this earth, I know it is going to be so wonderful when I leave. It's hard to think of leaving my husband, my mom, and my grandma, but it is going to be so sweet. Now, I am ready to go any day. I know that those same angels who came to comfort me would come to my family and comfort them. I would live on in their wonderful memories."

Tanya is also comfortable with the death experience. She notes, "One day I was swimming alone and my legs got tangled in the rungs of the ladder. I was stuck underwater and I could not get out. My head was down and my legs were up, trapped in the ladder. I panicked and lost all my air. All of a sudden everything was very quiet. A deep calm came over me and I wasn't scared at all. There was no sense of time. Everything was okay.

"It is not dramatic to die. There was an initial scary second when I panicked, but that was over very quickly. When the panic left I was surrounded with love and warmth. The next thing I knew, I was able to climb out of the pool, but as soon as I got out of the pool, I was afraid again. I never told anybody.

"Lately, I have been thinking a lot about this experience. Even though it was a long time ago, it was the first time I experienced the presence of my angels. I had the sense that they were there protecting me, even though I didn't actually pass over."

Like Lisa, Richard remembers making a choice. He tells us, "I had a stroke. During this time, before I woke up, there were two rectangular lights leading to two roads, side by side—everything else was dark—and I can remember being hesitant looking at them. I went over and looked at both roads and I knew that I had a choice to stay or go. Obviously I chose to stay. I felt very warm and good. There was no stress of any kind.

"Before this experience, I always had apprehension about dying. Now I am more at peace. Dying is no big deal and I feel better than I did before I made my choice to stay."

Kelly also remembers making a choice to stay. She notes, "At age 28, I required a pacemaker. After surgery, I developed an infection in my heart. While still dealing with the heart infection, I had two bouts of food poisoning. My body just couldn't take any more distress, and I was gravely ill. I remember praying, 'God, Jesus, or whoever is up there, I need answers. I can't keep going through this.'

"I then felt a presence of pure love enter the room. I fell asleep and left my body. I heard a loud hum like a radio frequency and saw a tunnel of pure white light. I felt as though I was sucked into a vacuum and came out into blue sky and white clouds where a fair-skinned man with brown hair and eyes stood looking at me. He was wearing a white robe trimmed in gold. He took me by my hands, and when I felt his touch it filled my soul with love and peace.

"He spoke to me without moving his lips and asked if I wanted to go with him or stay. I knew I had to stay to help others. He smiled, we laughed, and he let go of my hands. Suddenly I was back in my body and my friends were reviving me. Within three days, my heart infection and all other symptoms cleared up."

The will to live is the strongest will there is. Phyllis waited for a heart transplant for more than two years. The difficulty of finding a donor heart and sustaining a healthy life while you are waiting is enormously difficult. She had an indescribable will to live, even though death appealed to her and she wasn't afraid of it. During every moment she was aware that her life could be over that day. Each day, she waited—either for a heart or for death. There were no other choices for her.

She tells us, "I know what dying is! You simply go to sleep and wake up in a different place. Death has no pain. I always thought it would be painful—but you just want to go to sleep. Here are my thoughts and what I experienced when I was dying in the supermarket.

"I was walking down the aisle thinking, 'Oh, I don't feel good—but I haven't eaten—that's okay—where is the cheese? Oh there it is. How come I didn't see it? What is that light? God, I really need to lie down. I don't think I am going to get this done. Maybe I'll come back and finish later. I better get something to drink. I must get out of here. Oh, God. Okay, okay, I have to lie down. I need to lie down.

How am I going to check out my groceries? If I can just get up on the checkout counter and lie down!'

"Then I heard myself say to someone, 'Do you think you could call 911 for me? Don't worry about it, I can get into the ambulance.' Time was all distorted. Then the next thing I heard was, 'Cannot read . . . 40 over nothing.'

"'But there is no pain,' I thought. 'Gee, what nice people these are.' There was never panic or pain of any kind. I just wanted to go to sleep. I felt fine.

"People think it is black when you die. It isn't; it's white. When you die, you die from your highest place, not your lowest. It's a St. Louis moment, like stepping through the arches. When I was ill, I knew I went in and out of life. Today I know what a gift living is."

Phyllis still lives life moment-to-moment, not knowing what will happen next. She told us this part of her story from intensive care as she waited to see which would come first: a new heart—or death.

She continues, "After my episode in the supermarket, the doctors placed a combination pacemaker/defibrillator in my chest: a pacemaker to keep my heart beating in proper rhythm, and a defibrillator to give my heart a jolt of electrical current if my heart stops beating for longer than eight seconds.

"It's disconcerting when the defibrillator goes off. The machine buzzes first, then it zaps and sounds like an x-ray machine. When you feel the defibrillator go off, you know you would have died if it didn't work. The doctor can 'read' the exact times it went off. On the day they put me in intensive care to wait for a new heart, I 'died' twice. The defibrillator started my heart again.

"That night, terror started. I can't explain it. It was like there was no way out of this trip except to go through the horrible darkness to reach the other side. However, I discovered the terror was over once I made the final decision to go through with the heart transplant. By the morning I knew I was in for it all and that my decision was final until I died or got my new heart. There was no other choice but to believe. I had to!

"The angels are here. They told me that the man who is going to give me his heart finally made his decision that it is time for him to go. After they told me that, the terror is totally gone. His heart is being prepared for me.

"I don't know if angels get stronger or if it's my perception of them that gets stronger, but I sense that they have done all the planning that needs to be done. I am lying here in ICU because the machine keeps going off. It has gone off six times in a row after all these months, and I know it has happened because my new heart is ready. Everything is ready in my entire life for my new heart to come to me."

We wish all of you could meet Phyllis. She has made it through the surgery, and she is living life now with a quality and renewed purpose she never thought possible. It is as though a door that she could have gone through has closed, and now she has new work to do. She rejected the option to die.

Twelve

If It's Not Our Time

We are always loved and protected by God through His angels. If it is not our time to die, it simply will not happen.

Sometimes people don't even know the angels just saved their life. This probably happens more often than we will ever know. The stories included in this chapter show how it happens and how the life lessons involved have changed the individuals' paths. From these stories comes a greater understanding of the participants' own spirituality.

Dean begins, "When I was 16, I had a motorcycle accident. I don't remember the accident itself, but I was hit by a car, flew 30 feet in the air, landed on my head, and woke up in the hospital wondering where I was. My father was in the room with me when the doctor came in and told him that I probably wasn't going to make it. I heard the doctor say the whole thing, and I was thinking, 'What? That's not right. I'm still here!' I felt it was definitely not the right time for me to go into another dimension. I knew I wasn't going to die!"

Denise's angels stepped in to keep her and another woman out of harm's way. She says, "My car suddenly stopped on a rainy, cold day in October. All of a sudden the brakes made the most horrible sound, and the car stopped. I looked up and there was a lady with an umbrella crossing the road not six inches in front of my car! She did not even look up, but kept on walking. I was stunned and knew immediately that it was her angel, my angel, or both that stopped the car. I will never forget that blessing as long as I live, and I thank God and my angels for it often."

Judy G.'s story also involves a car traveling on a stormy night. She explains, "It had been raining off and on. I got off work at midnight, and my girlfriend picked me up in her car. Ten minutes later, we came to a very slick part of the freeway, and the car lost traction. My friend foolishly slammed on the brakes, and we started going in circles. We hit the curb, which sent us airborne. I yelled, 'Oh, God, don't let us die!' Two hands grabbed me by the shoulders and jerked me out of the front seat into the back seat. Actually, it seemed like I was watching myself go through the accident from outside the car. I could see myself from two places at once. I thought I was dead at 19.

"All of a sudden, I saw a man beside me. He was very large, and although I couldn't see all of him, I knew he was there to help me. He said, '*We have better plans for you than this. You must change your path.*' He hugged me, and left. Suddenly, I became aware that now I was on the floor in the back seat of the car, and that both my friend and I were fine.

"Everyone who saw the car later thought that people had died in the wreck. I could not believe it myself. There was no way we should have lived through it, but if God hadn't pulled me out of the front seat when I called on Him, I would be dead. I believe the man was God, and I listened to His warning. My life changed that night."

Many people are frightened when they have dreams about death, but it doesn't necessarily mean you are getting ready to make your transition. The symbolism of death in a dream can mean change, and how those changes occur are totally up to each individual. The "death" of something means the end of it. It could, perhaps, be an attitude, a belief, or a sense of self that you no longer need or that you are in the process of changing. It would be rare that a dream would be predicting your actual death. Sometimes a death dream is a warning to be aware, but usually a death dream is announcing the beginning of something new.

For about a month, Jeanne was dreaming and having premonitions that she was going to die. She even dreamed how and when she would die.

While Jeanne was at work, she had a cerebral hemorrhage caused by an aneurysm in her brain. Fortunately, the woman at the next desk knew what to do and immediately packed her head in ice. After Jeanne had been hospitalized for a week, an angel appeared to her husband and told him to move her from that hospital to Mass General Hospital. Her doctor was furious and said the change of hospitals could possibly kill her.

However, Jeanne was moved, and the doctors at Mass General did the most amazing surgery! Later, the doctor told Jeanne that she would be in rehab for at least a year, but in spite of some speech problems and a weakness on her left side, she walked out of the hospital one week later. Her neurosurgeon told her husband, "Thank the Man Upstairs for your wife's life. God guided my hands. There is no way I did this." Jeanne had less than a one percent chance of surviving and returning to full health, but today she is perfectly fine.

In addition, Jeanne says that during the surgery she did die! This is called a near death experience (NDE). She went to a place of great beauty where her dead relatives met her. She saw her father, her sister, and the grandparents she had never met in life. Jesus came to her, carried her in his arms, and told her it was not her time, and that she was to come back and finish her life and her work. But she did not want to come back!

After Jeanne was released from the hospital, she was angry and cried for months because she wanted to stay on the other side. Still, she remembered that she had been told she had a job to finish here on earth. When she and her husband compared notes, they realized that the angel who had appeared to him was the same angel who was with Jeanne the whole time she was unconscious. It gave Jeanne a wonderful feeling and a great sense of peace to know the same angel had helped both of them. She also knew that everything was perfect and that a new phase of her life had begun.

Thirteen

Living and Ethical Wills

A living will is a document that addresses the medical scenario a person wishes to have during an illness. Every adult, while they are healthy, should create a living will. A good idea is to make out one with your loved ones around the kitchen table. Everyone in the family will then have written down what they want and there will be no doubts if the living will is ever needed.

A good format to follow was created by the head of a not-for-profit group called Aging With Dignity. They call it the Five Wishes. Here are the major points.

Wish One: Who should make care decisions when you can't?

Wish Two: What kind of medical treatment do you want and what don't you want? Be specific.

Wish Three: How comfortable do you want to be? Do you want pain relief medication, even if it makes you drowsy?

Wish Four: How should people treat you? Do you want your hand held, or to die at home if possible?

Wish Five: What do you want your loved ones to know about you? With whom do you want to make amends?

You will need to appoint a person who can be a fierce advocate for your best interests. The agent you name must be an expert on what is important to you so discuss your will with him or her. Also make sure you get copies of your living will to your doctor and your lawyer.

Our good friend, Rabbi Judith Schindler, recently gave a sermon about ethical wills and about the value of leaving behind a legacy for those you love. Here is a portion of her sermon:

> One very important way to ready ourselves for the transition or death process is to leave a will to divide our possessions. Most of us manage that, though reluctantly. But a material will is not enough—ordinarily we think only of the sharing of our physical belongings. But there is something further we can and ought to share: our values and our fundamental beliefs.
>
> There was a story in the paper several years back of a Japanese airplane crash. The pilot struggled to keep the plain aloft despite technical difficulties. It took thirty minutes to crash to the ground.
>
> In the midst of the rubble were found many notes scribbled during those last frightening minutes. On these papers were notes to loved ones, words of farewell, expressions of love, sketches of valuable lessons the victims learned from their lives. It appears that human beings have a fundamental

need to leave behind a message identifying who they are and what their lives stood for.

For centuries, people from all walks of life have prepared for their day of death not only by writing a material will, but also by writing what is called an "ethical will." The slips of paper written by the passengers on that Japanese airplane were the beginnings of such wills.

An ethical will is a letter from a parent to a child, from one relative or friend to another, or even from a dying child to parents summing up the lessons that have been learned in life. Ethical wills can be in any form—some lines of poetry, a simple note, words on a page—that children or loved ones can one day hold as a tender record of wisdom. Such a will can pave the way for our loved ones when we are no longer there to usher them through the chaotic path of life. Some of you may have received an ethical will, not knowing how to label it.

Jacob Weinstein, who died in 1974, emphasized to his children the importance of Judaism and of family. In his will he wrote, "I know I cannot impose my values and judgements on you, but I can and do request that you not let this heritage go by default but that you study it, participate in it, and make your decision on the basis of knowledge as well as sentiment. You will find that Judaism may be a very real help in holding you together as a family."

Arthur Ashe, a great tennis champion, left his daughter an ethical will in a letter that he wrote to her when she was four years old. He told her that she should learn two languages and master at least two sports. He told her that it is important to have money, but it is also important that money not have her.

His letter also notes, "You must not let your skin color hold you back and you must not let your skin color push you forward." He ends his letter by saying, "Don't be angry with me if I am not there in person when you need me. Don't feel sorry for me that I am gone. When we were together, I loved you deeply and you gave me much happiness. Wherever I am, when you feel sick at heart and weary of life or when you stumble and fall and feel that you cannot get up again, think of me. I will be watching and smiling and cheering you on."

❧

AN ANGEL MESSAGE: The process of transition is as much for the living as it is for the one whose life is ending. Love lessons of great importance can be learned. Family bonds may be strengthened and faith deepened. Not all experiences are joyful, but each is special and unique. And, in each one of them we are there to help in every way. It is too important a time not to have hosts of angels present.

Fourteen

Joy in Passing

Sometimes the way people choose to leave is humorous. It is as though death is a grand experiment and they want to play around with the experience a bit before making the final leap to the other side.

Sally describes her mom's transition. "About two months before Mom's death, she began to slow down. She began to prepare us that the time was approaching. In early October, I moved in with her. What a precious time it was. I made cinnamon toast for her just like she had for me when I was a child and wasn't feeling well.

"About noon one day, I was in the kitchen and Mom was in her bedroom, at the end of a long hall. I heard her coming down the hall yelling, 'Sally, This is it! This is it!' When I came out of the kitchen, I saw her moving fast, with her walker, one arm pointing skyward.

"She was radiant. Her speech was distorted, and I thought she might have had a stroke. I began to cry, but she waved her arms for me to stop, while continuing to talk in indistinct words. I did clearly hear, however, 'This is wild. This is wild! You were right, the angels are here!' She was completely full of joy and laughter.

"My husband picked her up to take her back to her bedroom. She went down the hall in his arms, screaming with delight, 'Yahoooooooooo!'

"She continued to speak unintelligibly, but we began to hear what seemed like other languages. I think I heard what sounded like Swedish, or German, maybe Yiddish. I'm not certain. Later, my sister did some research, and *The Encyclopedia Britannica* captured perfectly what my mother was doing. The gift of tongues, it says, is 'utterances approximating words and speech, usually produced during states of intense religious excitement; and the speaker is considered to be in conversation with divine beings.'

"Sometime during the night she tried to leave her body by counting to three and lifting up. It's hard to explain, but it was another piece of that time. The room felt full of an energy that I can only describe as a thick presence of God. At dawn, Mom was still with us, giving us looks like 'I can't believe I am still here!' All of her loved ones were there. She entered a deep sleep, not to be wakened again.

"The next night, I dozed beside her bed. Then I felt the tap. It could have been only from her, on her way out, because no one else was in the room at that moment. Then the candle went out. That was the moment she went home to God."

Grace's experience involved an elderly friend and spiritual teacher who was in a nursing facility. She writes, "I knew she had only hours to live. Toward the end she told me she had dreamed she had crossed a small bridge to the other side and now she was back to tell me how beautiful it was over there. The thing I remember most was that she told me, 'They even have bread trees over there!' She crossed that bridge three times. The final time she told me that she would not be back, but would be with me always. She then passed on. This experience highlighted my life as I actually walked with her to the other side."

Yvonne W. remembers her wonderful, handsome, 84-year-old friend she called "grandpa" who loved to tell stories about his roots. She explains, "He talked about riding his horse in the mountains with his brother, Paco, and when they came home they would sit, talk, drink a cognac, and smoke a cigarette.

"'This is heaven to me,' he would say.

"Grandpa would pause with an ecstatic smile, and say, 'After that, I wouldn't care if I died.' We objected to the last comment. Grandpa raised his fingers to his lips to silence us. He then said somberly, 'Death is not a thing to be feared. Death is the best part of living because that is when we really get to go home. When I die, I hope it rains, so my trip to heaven can be refreshing.'

"A few months later, Grandpa went on his first vacation in 18 years, the last time I would see him alive. Mom and I were eating dinner when the phone rang. The caller related, 'Grandpa was so happy—telling us all about his visit as he smoked his cigarette and sipped a cognac. All of a sudden it was over.' On the day of his burial, there was a torrential downpour, ending a long drought."

The purpose of this chapter was to tell you not to be surprised if the one making their transition is ready to go and is eagerly looking forward to their passing. There is often a readiness that overrides the sadness of the event. "He was ready to go," is often said, and it is true.

Fifteen

Inner Knowing

Some people seem to know when they are going to die. It is almost as if they planned everything out for the convenience of family and friends. The whole process becomes almost an orchestration of events down to the tiniest detail.

Craig remembers, "My dad was going to work. He left the house at 10:00 P.M., and he beeped the horn like he always did to say goodbye. He was on the freeway, and then the car went onto the shoulder. He just kept slowing down and slowing down and slowing down and ended up in what looked like the weeds on the side of the freeway. Well, the man in the car behind Dad followed him because he thought something was definitely wrong. He pulled up behind my father, jumped out of his car, went to my father's door, and found that for all practical purposes my father was dead. Amazingly, the man who followed him off the road was the priest of the church my mom and dad attended. So he gave Dad last rites. In the meantime, a policeman saw the two cars and also thought something was wrong. He pulled right up behind the priest's car. The place where the car stopped was immediately across from the funeral home that took care of my dad's remains. It was uncanny how my dad seemed to 'arrange' to have the priest follow him to the funeral home when he passed over.

"Later, when my mother went to where my dad worked, she found that during the previous week, he had gone to human resources to find out what life insurance he had and how it was set up. Dad had anticipated the possibility of his death whether it was conscious or subliminal. Mother never knew he was feeling ill, or if he had a premonition, or anything else."

Denise's father also seemed to sense that transition was near. She says, "As if out of nowhere, my father began tying up the loose ends of his life. He taught my son (his only grandson) about the Battle of Iwo Jima, in which he fought during World War II. They watched movies, read books, and my son interviewed his grandfather on videotape. He inventoried his tools. My dad had been estranged from his father all of his life, but before passing on he took my son and me to my grandfather's grave.

"Preparations took him about a year before he began to look tired and gaunt. It was apparent he was preparing to go 'home,' and by May the signs were obvious that his time was very, very near. When we took him to the doctor, all the tests were negative. There was really nothing wrong with him. My father was not ill, but his soul was preparing to separate from his body. His spirit was ready, and nothing was going to stop it.

"The day that my father seemed to want to pass, my mother called all of the local children to his side. They kept waking him up, not allowing him to leave. His body had deteriorated to the point of where he had to be admitted to intensive care. Again, all the tests were negative. There was nothing wrong with him. After five days in intensive care, he was transferred to a nursing home. It took four days of getting him settled in before we would leave him alone at night. On the fourth night, he passed quietly in his sleep.

"That very afternoon, Dad's spirit came to me absolutely jubilant! It was difficult to cry at the funeral because I had this happy, bouncing spirit at my side giving me play-by-play of the 'other side' and how relieved he was to be out of his body. He spent his first few weeks in his new 'home' speaking to me daily. Now he shows up when I invite him, or when he has something that he wants to tell me. At Christmastime he gave me instructions for the assembly of a clear acrylic ball ornament filled with symbols of his life, as a gift for each of my five siblings and my mother. He even designed a crossword puzzle with clues about the symbols.

"I felt that I had time to grieve my father while he was alive and to help him prepare for his passing. From where he is now, he is much happier. On a selfish note, he is in a much better place to help me when I need him, too."

When Laurie R.'s father was dying, she told him, "You have one experience at this and I have one opportunity to make it the best experience possible for you."

She reflects, "Even now, after all this time, I have no regrets about his passing. I had called my friend who was a psychic and asked her what to do. Even though I knew it might ordinarily be out of my father's comfort zone, we were going to do what she said.

"She told me to put one hand over his heart chakra and one hand over his crown—I had never done anything like that before—and pray for healing, love, light, and energy. She said, 'I am not talking about healing his body; I am talking about healing his soul to enable him to move forward.'

"I did that as his body was shutting down. I could literally feel him pulling the energy from me when I put my hands on his body. I was glued to him. I was in this ultra place, and spiritual banter was coming forth from me. She had told me to encourage him to explore the white light—to go up to it and be a part of it; to get used to it. So I did. I kept telling him these things.

"When he did pass, my mother was asleep with her head on the bed holding Dad's hand. I woke her up, and told her it was time. When he heard her voice say goodbye, we both felt his spirit physically jump back into his body just for a minute. His heart rate returned to where it had been, and his oxygen levels went back to where they hadn't been in hours. It was like he came back for a second just to say, 'I know you're going to be okay. I'm going to go now.'

"My mother had never seen anyone die before. After it was over she raised her head and said, 'This isn't so bad. He had a good experience. Everyone should go this way.'

"We knew that the greatest gifts were to be part of someone's birth, or someone's passing. If you believe in God, you are between that person and God at that time, and that is pretty special!

"On the way home, I saw my Dad in the car out of the corner of my eye and heard him say very clearly, 'Thank you for setting me free.'"

Sixteen

Letting Go

There comes a time when caregivers and family members must let go. We knew a woman who, whenever it appeared that her mother was about to die, would carry on and scream and yell, "Don't go, Mother! Don't go!" The old lady kept living with constant care and great expense, finally dying at age 96. She had been bedridden and in and out of a coma for many years. She was ready. Her daughter wasn't.

Annie's account of how one's friends and family can help with the transition shows another way to face the inevitable. She begins, "I was 32 years old and I was eating breakfast with my mom. Suddenly, right before my eyes, Mom was having a stroke. Instead of having a panic attack, I went into clinical mode and the nurse in me took over. After I got her to the hospital, she was placed in an ICU unit.

"I had never met my deceased grandmother, but she was there, at the top of my mother's bed. She was looking after her child as she had done so many times before. There were other deceased relatives there as well. There was my grandfather, whom I call The Baron; my father, the man she pledged her love to for more than 34 years; and her cousin, whom she loved more than life itself. I noticed that they were all there to watch over my mom.

"I spent a good part of the day praying. Later, as I walked the hall by her room, I realized the deceased family members where still there. When I heard the doctor say to stop the CPR, I realized that all I wanted to do was go in with her and be with her one last time. I went in and asked the remaining nurse to leave me alone with my mother. I was not really alone, of course, because my deceased family was there with her. I saw Mother's soul get out of her body when my father offered her his hand. She looked back at me as if to say that she would stay if I needed her, and I told her that she needed to go with them. My grandmother called out to her daughter, 'Louisa,' and with that Mother left with her family.

"I am not sad because I know that my family was there to show my mother the way home, and that is something that gives me great comfort and joy. I believe that my mother and father, with the watchful eye of my grandmother, are guiding my every step to help me along life's path. She is still my mother, and she is still watching over me until it is her time to come for me."

Michelle also learned a strong lesson about love and letting go. She explains, "My friend was diagnosed with AIDS, and he was in the latter part of the disease. He had only one sister with him in New York City, so I tried to support him emotionally, and often went to the hospital to be with him.

"I was at a Broadway play one evening, and halfway through the performance, I felt his spirit or energy and heard his voice. I knew I had to go to the hospital to see him. I left the play, and as I walked into the hospital, the nurses said he was going. Only his sister was there at the time. I said to her, 'Maybe we should hold his hands.'

"Her reply was, 'Oh, no! He doesn't want to be touched.' I said again that I thought it would be a good idea to each take one of his hands. Now this was hard, because to me a dying person is a very scary thing. It's like holding the hand of death.

"The nurses were running around looking at things, and I began to pray and ask for the angels to guide me through this because I had no idea what to do. It was only about two or three minutes later that I felt warmth in my hand and in his. I asked his sister, 'Do you feel that?'

"She commented that she could feel his fingers moving, and I agreed with her. Then one of the nurses asked, 'What are you doing?'

"I told her we were holding his hand while he went through the death experience. The nurse replied, 'Well, you are bringing him back.'

"The monitors were registering his heart and other signs, and they were going up. She said, 'You want to let him go, not bring him back.'

"Then he started grasping at the sheets like he didn't want to go. I noticed he could move his hands, so I said, 'Jim, move your hands if you are feeling me.' Then we communicated through his hands, even though the nurses said he was really in a coma. I said, 'Jim can you feel this? It is amazing! It feels so good!' Jim kept squeezing my hand.

"His sister was very, very afraid, and said, 'I don't think we should be doing this.' Suddenly, a few other friends came into Jim's room, and I asked them all to take each other's hands as we surrounded Jim. As we did this, he started to relax from a place of gripping pain. I asked the angels to come. I knew his mother came from the other side. I could tell she was there. I asked if he saw her, and he squeezed my hand.

"I was divinely asked to lead him into the other side. I told him that we were going to surround him with love and light and lead him over. I actually felt like I was going with him, which was very bizarre. In fact, I had the knowing that the angels thought I was coming with him! I kept saying, 'Not me. Just him!' At the end he was smiling when he let go of my hand. Then, he was gone. The experience of his passing was so great, so warm, and we were all so ecstatic that we couldn't believe it. Then everyone sort of hugged each other. Jim was a beautiful man.

"Jim inspired me to write so much that I filled an entire journal after his death. For a while, I felt like he was right beside me, and it was really uncomfortable. Later, when I was ill with a terrible headache and praying for relief, Jim came to me and said, 'I can't believe you are ignoring me! You have people to help you!'

"Jim's death experience changed my life. His energy was tangible. I will never question the power of God again."

We asked Sidney, who has worked for many years with people in transition, to comment on the dying process from his experience and knowledge. He begins, "In working with the energetic bodies of people who are dying, I have noticed that a shift happens at some point that tells everyone it is okay to go. I had a client whose parent was not lucid. The children had to make the decision that extraordinary measures were not in the best interest of their dad or their family. Although their dad was unable to speak audibly, somehow he communicated to his children that he was ready to go. All the family members seemed to receive the message at the same time. Somehow, somewhere, maybe from their inner knowing, everyone knew that there was a better place for their father to be—now. It was time for their dad to go.

"Medical professionals can keep you alive, but when the angels have spoken, it's okay to go, and everyone knows it's okay—including medical personnel, family members, and their supporters. They will know also when it's time to go to a hospice facility, to the hospital, even to remove life support. There may be grief and pain when that time comes, but there need be no regrets for the life that has been lived.

"In the hospital or hospice experience, both the patients and the family are scared at first! Fear of the unknown is a big part of the atmosphere. However, energy changes as one gets comfortable with the death process. Feeling scared gives way to a peaceful acceptance.

"Shifts occur when death is imminent. Passing becomes okay. There is another shift of energy when death actually occurs. After the person dies, the energy of the deceased changes, of course, as well as the family in grief, and the hospital personnel. The energy becomes comforting, loving, and tender at a depth one does not normally experience.

"When death actually occurs, energy leaves the body and spreads out—not just up. It fills the space and beyond. The energy that is everywhere becomes a part of everything. When we die, we become part of the space that is between everything. We become part of thought instead of solid matter. But our energy also can be collected up, back into the shape of our body, like a hologram—a three-dimensional portrait of collected energy. This collective form of energy benefits humans so we will know who is communicating with us. A deceased person is still a part of everything. We can hear their thoughts, and they can hear ours."

⁂

AN ANGEL MESSAGE: Birth . . . choice. You, as a soul, are given the right to pick when you are born and the lessons you want to learn in your lifetime. You choose the proper circumstances so that you may accomplish everything you need to accomplish. When, where, how . . . all are up to you.

Death . . . choice. You, as a soul, are given the right to pick when you are finished with your lessons. God and your soul know when your work is through, and you may go back to Heaven. That is all. Not exactly an eight-hour day, life, but it is certainly the best work you could ever do.

Life is good. Death is good. They are the same.

Part III

The Other Side: Beyond Transition

Peace. Peace. Peace!
This is the ultimate place of peace!
. . . the angels

It was a very happy day when we went into New York City to meet with our editor and to see our completed book, *Angelspeake: How to Talk with Your Angels*, for the very first time. We took the train from Trudy's home in Connecticut and were walking along 5th Avenue when we decided to stop at Brentano's Bookstore to ask if our book was listed in their computer. We thought it was too soon for it to actually be on the shelf because our publication date was still several weeks away. Much to our joy, it was there in Brentano's computer! Here we were, two mature women, dancing all over the bookstore, giving each other high-fives and hugs and telling everyone we were published authors!

We left the store with thankful hearts singing and walked arm in arm down 5th Avenue, knowing our angels surrounded us, and that our deceased mom and dad were between us. We knew it! There wasn't a doubt in our minds that they were there sharing our joyous moment, a moment we will never forget.

Sensing the presence of a departed loved one is not an unusual occurrence. We have heard from many people who have been contacted by loved ones who have passed over, sometimes in writing, like we teach, and other times by events like a door slamming at a certain moment, a significant picture falling over, or a song on the radio stirring a memory. We have heard about several "knocking" incidents when no one was visibly there. No matter what the event or how insignificant it may have seemed to anyone else, the person having the experience knew it was a message from the other side.

Occasionally people become frightened when a deceased relative appears or starts communicating with them in some way. Sometimes our reaction may be from guilt, because we think of the things we didn't do, could have done, or should have done while they were alive. But the common experience of everyone who has a spiritual encounter with a deceased person is love. LOVE.

Our angels told us, "*When souls go to heaven, they are only love. That is all they can be.*"

After a person dies, they become part of the light. They become connected to a divine source that only loves. Even if they were not happy people on earth, the parts of their character that were unloving, unhappy, dishonest, mean, or unforgiving do not go to the other side. Souls return only as the love they are.

Just because a person dies, doesn't mean you lose the relationship. Most often, loved ones will return at first to assure you they are okay, to help alleviate your grieving, or to comfort your sorrow. You feel their love, even if no words are spoken. Love surrounds the whole experience, and through love, healing takes place.

This section is devoted to the wonderful stories we have heard from people who knew that their loved one was near.

Seventeen

Feeling Their Energy

There are many ways your loved ones may come to you, but the most common way is to feel them. Your loved ones may also speak to you or write to you. They may come in dreams. But however they choose to communicate, you will know *who* it is, and you will know *why* they came. You will not doubt it.

Carol's dad first came to her while she was reading our book. She writes, "This is the first time I had an experience like this. I was distraught over the way he suffered in the hospital before he died, and as a nurse, I felt I let him down. When I read that any bad feelings, negativity, or pain does not transfer to the other side, I thought of Dad's horrible suffering as his lungs filled with fluid. With that thought I started crying. Then, something that I can only describe as 'sand' came rushing toward me. It totally wrapped around me, inside and out. In my mind I heard myself say, 'Dad!' No words were spoken, but I was assured that he was okay! He was happy and things were good. It was the most beautiful, warm, peaceful experience of my life. I know now that my dad is at peace, and so am I."

Donna K.'s dad also paid her a visit after he died. She remembers, "The night before my dad's funeral, I was dozing off when my dad buzzed in. He reminded me of a bee buzzing around. I couldn't see him in the dark room, but I definitely 'felt' an image of him smiling with a creamy haze behind him. Mentally, I said hello, and that I loved him. Although he wasn't actually talking, I could hear him anyway. He said he was really busy, that there was so much to do, and he was in a hurry. I got an impression that he needed to research some things and then set some records straight. I had a vision of really big, old books that he needed to complete his research. He seemed so excited!

"One good thing about that visit is that I know he can move very fast. After seeing him zoom away, there is no question that if I need his support, it will be instantaneous. Just now while writing this, I was at a loss for words and asked him to help me remember what he said about being busy, and here he is helping me. Thanks, Dad. Oh yes, he wants me to be sure to tell you that because of his bravery in World War II, he was buried in Arlington National Cemetery. He is very proud of that."

When Gail's husband, Shannon, died, he left her his sheet-metal business. And he kept an interest in its outcome. She explains, "It was difficult for quite awhile since I did not know how to run the business. Once, while being audited, we were looking everywhere for papers the auditor needed. No one knew where the papers were. We tore the place apart looking for them. When we came into the office the following Monday morning, the papers were sitting in the middle of my desk. We asked everyone where they had come from, but no one knew. I believe the only place they could have come from was Shannon!

"On another occasion, I was bidding a job that was a type I had never done before. I had no idea how to do it. I put together an estimate, believing it would have to do. Suddenly, a tree standing in the corner of my office fell over, and the thought came to me that I should increase the estimate, which I did. Needless to say, we not only were awarded the contract, but we also made a fair profit on our work.

"I went to see Shannon every morning while he was in the hospital. One day when I got there, he said, 'Am I dead?' I told him no, and he said, 'Are you sure? I could swear I was dead. I was up floating around on top of my body, and I thought I was probably dead.'

"Now we just know he is there with us in the shop every day. We can feel him in the building. Some of the guys in the shop get scared, but we just tell them, 'Relax, it's Shannon.' We are used to it now. He was—and still is—always here, and he has taught me the parts of the business I didn't know so I could run it after he died."

Eighteen

Hearing Them

Nearly everyone has had the experience of hearing their name called loudly when no one was there. Perhaps you have heard voices or words in your head telling you to do something. You are not alone in your experience. Those on the other side communicate often with us to instruct, warn, comfort, or direct the living one.

Kaye heard her mother's voice just when she needed comfort. She explains, "The night before Thanksgiving, I was sitting in the kitchen sobbing my eyes out. A close friend had upset me terribly. As I was drinking coffee and crying so hard, I looked up and said, 'Mom, I wish you were here to help.'

"All of a sudden my mother's voice came loud and clear from the hallway. She said, 'Kaye, it's okay. Everything will be all right.' My mother had passed away in May, and this was my first holiday without her, but there she was, telling me it was okay. Her voice came from her bedroom down the hall, where she had passed away. Now, whenever I need comfort, I go to her room to talk with her. I feel her loving arms around me. Ten days before she died, she said that she would always be with my family and me, and that she would never leave us. That's a promise she has kept."

Al J. had a similar visit from his friend Mike. He shares, "On Christmas Eve I was laughing and talking on the phone with my best friend, Mike. By Christmas morning, he was dead from a car crash. I could not believe it and did not want to believe it. I went to my bedroom to pray, and while I was praying for Mike, I felt a hand on my left shoulder, and then a rush of warm energy from my head to my toes. At that moment I said, 'Mike, is that you?'

"I heard a distinct 'Yes.' I shall never forget that moment of his presence. I knew he had come to me to say goodbye."

Pat's husband, Curly, continues to boost her confidence now that he's died. She explains, "Two weeks before Curly died, he reviewed with me all our finances, investments, and the checkbook, and I said, 'Oh, how am I going to handle this without you?' Curly said I would have no problems because I had a very good business mind and I would get along just fine. Now that he's gone, whenever I have to make a financial decision, Curly is right there, saying, 'You can do it. There is no problem; you have a good mind to do that.' He keeps coming back to me to help and restore my confidence.

"Curly came to me in the shower once after he died. The showerhead wasn't working very well. I said, 'Curly, you left me without teaching me how to take this showerhead off.'

"He said, 'Don't worry, honey, I'll help you with it. But remember you have a heavy hand. Just do it lightly.' He guided me through taking off the showerhead, cleaning it, and putting it back on. It worked just fine after I cleaned it.

"Curly doesn't come back to me as often as he used to. It is as though he knows I have built my own life and have more confidence now, so I don't need him as much."

Often there is unfinished business when people die. It is not unusual for the departed one to come back and finish it. Linda's dad did just that. She remembers, "About two weeks after my dad's death, I was going to sleep one night and I heard him call my name. I asked, 'What is it?'

"Dad said, 'You have to go help your mother with her paperwork. She is not finding some important papers.' Because I had grown up in that house, and I was sad because he wasn't there, I didn't go. A couple of weeks later, he called on me again. In his exasperated voice, he said, 'Linda Lee, go help your mother! There are three life insurance policies she hasn't found!' I went and found them.

"My daughter told me the other night that she knew that Grandpa was around a lot. I dream about him, and the other night in my dream, I told him how much I loved him and miss him. He smoked cigars and pipes, and even now, when he is around, I smell them."

Deb Herman's message from her father came in the form of a dream. She told us, "My father was a true maven of the stock market. He was not impetuous, but had a knack for choosing long-term stocks that would always create cash. Although he was far more ill than he even knew, he was calling his broker and working deals almost to the very end. It was no wonder then, that one of his first contacts to me after his death was to give me a great stock tip.

"My father was always concerned about my financial status. I am not known in the family for my financial acumen. One night I had a very vivid dream in which my father got right in front of my face. We were nose to nose and he kept saying to me, 'buy AOL, buy AOL.' I remember saying in the dream that I knew nothing about stocks and had never invested in my life. He adamantly replied, 'Trust me. Buy AOL.'

I knew better than to argue when he is in one of those moods even if he is on the other side. What was most interesting is that his stock tip came before the stock split and before there was any announcement of a merger with Time Warner. I bought the stock and am still holding tight. I wonder if his tip could be considered insider trading?

Nineteen

Recognizing Signs

We have heard from many who have a strong sense that their loved ones have given them a sign they are there. When the stories are related to others, often they sound trivial, because the actual sign only had significance to the receiver. But the common comment is always the same: "I just knew it was . . ." Knowing is reason enough to believe.

Donna S. offers some ideas on how to recognize the signs. She begins, "To communicate with the soul of a loved one, ask before going to sleep to talk to that soul. Record your dreams when you wake up in the morning. Messages can manifest themselves in many forms; something you read, hear on the radio, or see on the television screen. Messages are always there; you just have to be open to receive them.

"One night, while I was lying in bed worrying about the bills and the telephone calls I hadn't made, I swore I heard my deceased son, Avery, whisper in my ear, 'Lighten up, Mom!' I laughed. I knew Avery was watching over me."

Paulette's sign took the form of a familiar calendar. She recalls, "My parents contacted me one day when I was going to the cemetery to put flowers on their graves for their birthdays. While I was en route to the cemetery, I asked for a sign that my parents were with me. I felt compelled to stop at a field where a woman I knew, named Jackie, was selling mums. When I stopped to purchase the flowers, Jackie said that she had a calendar for me that she had purchased at a garage sale. I knew exactly what she was talking about. It was the same calendar that my family had given away every year. It had bible verses and religious pictures on it. I knew that it had been sent from my parents in answer to my request for a sign that they were with me."

Carla's family took comfort in the presence of a butterfly. She writes, "After my father died, there was a persistent little butterfly that hovered in my mother's private courtyard behind her condo. Mom felt that this butterfly was connected to the spirit of my deceased father. The butterfly stayed until the day of their wedding anniversary and her favorite flower in the courtyard bloomed . . . out of season."

Urve's mother also paid her a visit after her death. Urve notes, "Before my mother died, she complained to me about the loose handle on my coffee table. She wanted me to fix it! Three or four days after she passed, I heard the handle rattle really loud. I went to see if anyone was there, and no one was! Then I felt a very strong presence of my mother, and I knew that she had come to say good-bye to me. I told her to fly and be free of her old, sick body, and I bid her goodbye. I felt better after this."

Marie was also comforted by the presence of her husband, Rob. She recalls, "My husband died suddenly two years ago, leaving me with a two-month-old daughter. Needless to say, it was a difficult time for me. One night I was lying in my bed crying and had my daughter next to me. As I was crying, I felt Nicolette touch my cheek, but it felt like an adult's hand—definitely not an infant's. It immediately brought me comfort. I knew Rob was there."

Twenty

Visitations

When someone who has died appears in front of you, it can be pretty shocking! However, no one we talked to seemed to feel anything but love and happiness when it occurred. After the initial shock, people talk about how happy the deceased person looks. The feeling is of love and joy, and the memory is treasured forever.

When Opal's mother was dying, she worried that she would be thrown into a lake of hellfire and brimstone. "I don't think so," Opal told her, "but after you die, if there is any way that you can let me know that I am right, then please do that."

Opal recalls, "After the funeral, my sister-in-law and I went back to the house. I was sitting on a chair in the living room and she was on the sofa. I felt a hand on my hair as we were talking. I used to calm down my mother by stroking her hair really gently. I looked up, and there stood my mother, looking young and beautiful, with a smile on her face. She looked like she did when I was a kid. I started to rise up, and she disappeared. My sister-in-law said, 'You don't need to say a word. I saw her, too.'"

Debbie C.'s grandfather continued to look after her cousin after his death. She reports, "My grandfather was a farmer and would walk from his place, across a field, to my cousin's house every day to check on her. She was fine and healthy. He did it because he wanted to. The day after our grandfather died, my cousin awoke to see him sitting on the side of her bed. He said, 'I just came to make sure you were okay.' She began to cry. He put his hand on hers and said, 'I'll always be here to make sure you are okay. I love you.'

"She replied, 'I love you, too, Grandpa.' Then he got up, walked out the back door, and moved across the field toward his house as she stared out the window and watched him go. When Grandpa reached the middle of the dirt road that ran between the two houses, he stopped, and a bright beam of light shot up into the heavens. He was gone."

Myrna was surprised by a visit from her late husband. She recalls, "I woke up one morning thinking about my husband, who had died several years before. All of a sudden he appeared by my bed. Everything was so natural. He had on a short-sleeved shirt, and he looked so happy. He was looking down at me with his wonderful smile like he adored me. I felt his love. I thought that maybe I would get a better look at him and opened my eyes a little wider. He was still there, but saw me looking, and he jumped back with a smile on his face and then disappeared. It was a wonderful experience and I treasure it."

Rev. Sally has been widowed twice, and both husbands have paid a visit. She explains, "My first husband, Al, and I were at the end of a long divorce when he was killed in an auto accident. At one point, when he wanted us to get back together, he told me that someday I would receive a check in the mail for a lot of money and that it would be from him.

"When he died, we were not on very good terms. A month later, after his death, he appeared at the foot of my bed and told me that he loved me. What he said was very comforting, and it gave us closure, but it was unnerving to have him appear that way. A few weeks later I received a check for $23,000 from an insurance company. I didn't even know he had a policy.

"My second husband, Stan, died after we were divorced for seven years. One night Stan and Al both came to talk to me. They told me they were doing fine. Then they let me know they were proud of me and how I was handling life and raising my daughter. They had become spiritual pals!"

Two years after John's mother died, she paid him a visit. He writes, "I was visiting my father, and I chose to sleep the first night on a small bed in my father's room. In that relaxed state between awake and asleep, I had a clear image of my mother as she looked during the thirty years I knew her. Mother appeared slightly above me and about ten feet away. She was clothed in white, and only visible from the chest up. There was an aura of soft white light around her. I didn't see her lips move, but in her normal voice she said to me, 'Take care of Daddy.' Then she was gone. The next day I told the others about the visit, and we concluded it must have been a brief dream from which I quickly awoke.

"Eighteen years later, I had open-heart surgery. My wife was sitting with me as I started to rouse from the deep anesthesia. I remember feeling an incredibly deep exhaustion. I just wanted to slide backward, as I would if I were floating on my back in a swimming pool. As I felt myself start to let go and slide backward, I was jolted by the same image of my mother that I had seen eighteen years earlier—an identical vision. As before, I saw no movement of her lips, but in the stern, scolding voice she sometimes used with me when I was a young child, she said, 'Now you stop thinking like that and do what you are supposed to do.' I abruptly stopped slipping away and soon awakened fully. This time I know it was not a dream or hallucination and that I would have died without her guidance.

"Mother has never appeared to me since that second visit, but I am greatly comforted to know that she still watches over me."

Lisa's grandmother received a comforting visit from her husband when her son died. Lisa explains, "My father died suddenly of a heart attack when he was 47. We did not call Grandma immediately because my uncle wanted to drive to her house to tell her in person. Before he arrived, Grandma awoke and became frightened because she sensed a man lying next to her. She was afraid, but in an instant she realized her late husband, who had died years earlier, was lying next to her.

"A great calmness came over her. Grandpa told her that everything was going to be all right and asked her not to worry. 'All will be well and everything is as it should be,' he said. He did not tell her that her son had died. In the morning, my uncle arrived and told her the bad news of my father's death. Of course she was devastated, but the vision or experience with my grandfather and his words of assurance sustained her in later days."

Diane's father passed away in December and paid her a visit that same night. She recalls, "As he was walking through the kitchen, he collapsed and died from a massive coronary. I heard the news of his death at 6:20 P.M.

"About 11:00, I was sitting on the couch trying to deal with my feelings, when my father came to me, sat in my green chair, and talked. He told me not to fear death and that I must be strong. He warned me that my sister would attempt suicide, and he told me where to look for her to save her, because it was not her time yet. He told me he had spoken to my brother, but he was unable to handle the experience. Dad asked me to try to explain to my brother that our dad was all right. He told me to watch out for certain things that would happen, and to be strong so I could handle specific affairs. Everything he told me did indeed happen just as he said it would.

"Everyone came to our house for a reception after the funeral. The fire alarm in our town went off while we were serving food. My dad had been fire chief for several years. Shortly after the alarm went off, our phone rang. The fire was at the home of one of our guests, and her husband and children were at home asleep. When she rushed home, she was grateful to learn that her family was safe. They told her that my father had awakened them and got them safely out of the house. Another man swore that he had seen my father at the fire, even though we all knew we had buried him that morning. I guess Dad had some unfinished business to attend to before his soul was actually able to pass over.

"I am not fearful of death now and have found a sort of peace with it. I realize this story may sound bizarre, but it happened as I have explained it. I was fully awake, not dreaming, and fully aware of my surroundings. I believe he came to me to try to reduce my fear and anxiety. He also needed me to put a stop to the events that could have added a great deal of unnecessary stress to what was already a very stressful situation in the family."

Twenty-one

Listen and Talk

One of the most common ways for someone on the other side to appear is in your dreams. Sometimes the experience seems more like an altered state of consciousness than a dream. There is more of a "real" feeling than a normal dream state, and there is a stronger sense of the person actually being there. Afterward the memory doesn't seem to fade as dreams do.

Kathleen's friend Lois heard from her mother in a dream. Kathleen writes, "The night of my son Nate's memorial service, I talked about communicating with people on the other side. Lois, a member of my yoga class, had lost her mother about six months before my son died.

"A few months after the service, Lois came to me and said, 'I have something to tell you, but I want to preface it first. This is just to let you know that I don't believe in spirits, I don't believe in the other side, and I don't believe in anything that you said the night of the memorial. Last night I had a dream that the phone rang. I picked it up and heard my mother's voice. The voice said, 'Lois, I am fine.' I know that it was my mother. The reason I am telling you this is because I never thought such a thing was possible."

Like Lois, Jim was able to visit with his father in a dream. He explains, "Five or six months after my dad died, I was taken to see him one morning before I woke up. A dark-haired lady with curls on the sides of her cheeks took me into black space. I was conscious of going through space very rapidly. Earth was just a dot. We arrived in front of a very large, brightly lit window. Dad and other members of the family were on the other side. Dad was seated with other family members standing behind him, and he had on a beautiful white toga. They were all dressed similarly. Dad said, 'Son, I feel better than I ever felt in my life.' He looked to be about 25 years old, but he was 63 when he died. I said to the lady who was guiding me, 'My, doesn't he look good?'

"I knew *I* wasn't dead. I never saw the lady's face; I saw only a side view of her. It was like I knew her. She seemed familiar, but I didn't get a name. I wish I had looked better at the people who were with Dad, but I didn't. Yet I know they were members of my family."

Lisa met her brother in a dream shortly after he died of a heart attack at age 45. She writes, "A few days later I 'dreamed' that someone unknown (maybe my guardian angel) took me to heaven to show me that my brother was okay. I stood in a corner with this person and watched my brother (who looked 17 and was dressed in a white shirt and tie) sitting at a round table with other people. They were greeting 'newcomers' and processing them to make them feel at home.

"My brother was never aware of my presence that I know of, and this part of the dream bothered me because I wanted him to know that I loved him and missed him. But the dream left me feeling that he was okay and that he was doing what he wanted to do. My brother was a great artist, and if heaven has a need for artists, which I suspect it does, then he is one of the lead artisans."

Twenty-two

Messages from Beyond

At some point in our gathering of stories about transition, we began to hear of people who had received messages from their deceased loved ones and had been overwhelmingly helped by the contact. It was as though the final goodbye had never really been said and the after-death communication, being unexpected and surprising, was profoundly moving.

One day Donna D., whose story about her husband's death appeared in *The Angelspeake Book of Prayer and Healing*, went to his gravesite to be with him. While she was there, she began to receive a message from him, as she had been taught to do in the book. She found some paper in her purse and wrote down the message she was receiving. This is part of what she received from him that day.

It begins, "It feels good to have you near me, dear wife. Perhaps this is more symbolic for me than for you. This is our private place—a place where we can meet. When you come here, you think of only spending time and energy with me. It is an honor and a pleasure and a joy to have you all to myself and not have to share you with the rest of the world—I should say universe. Today is a good day to die. As a matter of fact, any day is a good day to die! Isn't that funny? You see, you can never take anything too seriously, not even death. As long as you take life and all its experi-ences as joy, learning, going forward, and loving, you'll never fear death because you will—no matter what time it comes—accept it.

"Well, my love, you look great! You're on your way to your new life. Enjoy it, for I will be with you to make sure you are loved. For you deserve nothing less than to be loved for your beauty and your heart.

"Dear heart, now I too ask for your forgiveness, for not sharing my life with you more. We might have had a differ-ent life. Not that I didn't have a wonderful life with you, but I could have had more; more of everything if I would have taken the time to understand how much you truly loved me.

"I now know and don't ask me why I didn't realize it at the time. You would have gone to the edge of the earth for me, and I am so honored that you loved me to that extent. There I was, the luckiest man on earth and I didn't even realize it. Well, my love, you had perfect timing. You arrived with your beautiful flowers; you stood on my headstone like I asked, and you spent time with me; time that was only for me. Thank you! Thank you! Thank you!

"You are my very precious love. Take care as you go. I will be with you in love and light. You are my angel on earth.

"All my love, Ralphie"

Barbara H., Margie, and Joe received a message from their father on the day their mother died. Barbara H. explains, "Our mother had been in a coma for more than three weeks. We kept thinking, 'Where there's life, there's hope,' but it was becoming more obvious that she wasn't going to make it. The morning our mother passed over, we found a fax on Joe's machine. It was from Marianne, a very spiritual friend of Joe's wife, Helen, who is from Australia. We had not been in touch with her for several years. Her comment on the fax was, 'I don't know what is happening in your life, but I felt I should pass this message on to you. I received this from my spirit guides.'

"The message read, 'Hello, Dear Marianne, this is Joe's father, and my message to Joe and Helen is one of patience. Please be patient, Joe, as your mother is processing her life and finding the courage to move across to me and life once again in spirit. She has the fear of letting go and the fear of what is to come. I am waiting so patiently for her and when she is ready, she will come. Please allow her the good grace to acknowledge her life in the physical and to let go now of all her disappointments and her failures, along with her joys. You both still have much to do, and in her going, you will release a burden and responsibility.

"'Much love and honor, Dear Ones.

"'Dad in Spirit with many hugs for you both.'

"Three hours later, Mother passed away. Afterward we were very happy to know that Mom and Dad are together again after so many years."

Elspeth, an e-mail friend of ours from Scotland, had a message from her father. His love for her just jumps out of his message.

"Hello, my Sunshine. The love that we shared on the earth cannot be broken. It is now magnified even more. It was the purest unconditional love you and I shared. We were one. You knew that. I told you before I died that you couldn't keep me here and I would be of more use to you on the other side. I think you can see the reasons why, now, even though you didn't at the time. It is all becoming clear for you as you become even more connected to spirit.

"I am so proud of you and what you are doing. You are on your chosen path. That is why you had *me* because it was me who helped wake you up to your work and the spiritual learning you had to achieve this lifetime. The angels love you so dearly for your contact with them and also for all the work you have done with others in such a short time. You will continue to do more workshops in the future. There are many benefits. You and Barbara and Trudy will all work together."

Her father then offered this reasurring poem:

Sisters of Love

Sisters of Light

Heaven brought you together.

To bring a planet into Light.

We were so touched by the messages people were receiving, we decided to call up our own mother. Her death had been a long one, and during her last months she was unable to speak and was in and out of consciousness. Our last recollection of her was of an emaciated woman in pain— no longer the mother we had known. We thought that would be our last memory of her. When we wrote to her, we were able to create all new memories of love. Best of all, we were also able to understand that even though her dying process had looked horrible, it really wasn't from her point of view. We were greatly comforted.

Here is her message to everyone who must help their own parent die.

"I 'died' long before I died. My death was a long and complicated one, which took many years, yet each stage was important to the healing and to the lessons I needed, and for the lessons of my children. This message is for you who must watch your mother die by inches and who must agonize as each breath comes one after another. This message is for you who pray that each breath be the last and that each breath will finally finish the life you have loved no matter how your relationship has been. For when the final breaths do come, there is only love between the soul dying and the soul living. As you hold the hand of your mother, there is only unconditional love, and your prayer for her death is the truest, most loving gift you can give her. She welcomed you into the world with birth, and you are finalizing the gift by giving her back to the place from which you came.

"When you were born, at that moment, there was only hope for your future. Mothers pray that their child be happy and safe while living his or her life, and at the moment of death, that is what you wish most of all for your mother. Believe that she is going to a happy and safe place.

"Do not be afraid to let her go, for many times she has already left. When the cancer hit my brain, for the most part I was not there. I was not 'stuck' there anymore. I could leave at the will of my 'deep brain.' Look into the eyes of your loved one. You will see her presence, or you will not. If there is no one 'home,' know that the soul is hovering close by, but not necessarily in the body, for the body is no longer a suitable house. As long as there is breath, there is still a type of attachment, but there is not a 'stuck' soul in an unusable body. A soul is free. A body is confinement. A sick body is a lesson point for all who are involved, but not necessarily a housing for the soul.

"I was not in pain! My body felt pain. My soul did not. I only felt love."

Twenty-three

Making Amends

Our Uncle George was a terrible tease. When we were little, he babysat for us sometimes, and one of his favorite things to do was to put us in the closet and lean on the door so we couldn't get out. Today, it would be considered abusive, but then it was just called "Uncle George's weird sense of humor." Trudy was particularly affected by this form of "humor" and later in life had a great deal of trouble with claustrophobia.

After Uncle George had been dead for some years, he came to Trudy one time as she was having a healing session. He apologized to her for his actions and helped cure her, right then, of her claustrophobia. It was a very important, healing event. Trudy is finally clear with Uncle George and can now live comfortably when faced with tight situations. It was a posthumous "I'm sorry."

Our father didn't come to us for many years. Then he came under unusual circumstances. He loved baseball more than anything, and he was truly an expert on the game. Now, when Barbara goes to a Padres game she feels our dad there. Amazingly enough, it also happens that there is always an empty seat beside her. She calls it "Dad's seat." Why not?

Like Uncle George, Beverly H.'s father also appeared with an apology. She begins, "First a little background. When I was a teenager, I wanted desperately to go to Woodbury College in Los Angeles to study fashion design. My dad wanted me to go to San Diego State and get a regular degree. He won out.

"Lately I have been having flashes of dress designs that I strongly feel I must create. Then I got this message from my dad, who died ten years ago. He said, 'I'm watching over you. You are okay. Take lots of time for thinking. You have some very good ideas. Plan carefully and all will work out for you. I'm sorry I took you off your path so many years ago. I tried to see myself in you. I wanted for you what I needed for myself.

"'Now you can fulfill the dream. It's a better time and a better plan. You don't need to go to school in order to express your natural talent. People will accept your creations far and wide. Bring your daughter into the business. She's more people-smart than you are, and it will be rewarding for her, too.

"'Keep calling your mother. She needs you. She's not as strong as she thinks she is. Take care of yourself. You have much to live for.'"

Oftentimes, people who had difficulty expressing how they felt when they were alive have no trouble at all sharing their love now that they are in spirit. In fact, it seems that the whole reason the deceased one wanted to communicate was to make absolutely sure their family members knew how dearly they were loved.

Taylor asked her mom if she could hear her. She received this assurance and apology: "Yes, I can hear you. Thank you for asking me. I love you. I want you to know that I have always loved you. I need to tell you that I am sorry for our misunderstandings. I realize that you love me too, and you took care of me. I realized then that I was wrong about you. I thought you would abandon me, but I was wrong. You did very well. Everyone did, and I thank them.

"I have found peace. Please tell everyone for me. I would like you to keep reaching out to the family. Try to get them together again. Keep trying."

Patty's dad contacted her to straighten out some unfinished emotional business. His message begins, "There are so many things I wanted to tell you but due to the condition I was in, I wasn't able. I want first to tell you how much I love all of you and thank you for everything you did for me all those months. I could hear you crying out to God, asking that He restore my health, but I knew that it was not meant to be.

"There were many things I did during my life on earth that hurt the ones I loved most dear, and I regret those things. If only I could have let you each know just how much I did regret what I had done and asked for your forgiveness, but my physical and mental state didn't permit me to.

"I wanted to be able to provide so much more for you than I was able to. I worked very hard and in a physically demanding job during my lifetime. The money I earned wasn't always shared as equitably as it should have been. I spent my money on things that benefited me. You have great business sense. Take what has been left to you and use it to its fullest potential. It is a pittance compared to what you deserve.

"Know that I love you and that this gift that I had wanted to give you for so long could only happen through this end. Think of your old man every once in a while and say thank you."

The healing in these contacts with deceased ones is amazing! The wounds of generations of families who were unable to express their feelings while they were on earth are healed by a message from the other side. Burdens are lifted. Love transcends death, and pure love is felt by all participating souls—on both sides.

Bob wrote the following note to his dad, who had been killed, along with Bob's sister, Carolyn, in the Tet Offensive in Vietnam in 1968. It begins, "Dear Dad, I can't believe I am trying to reach you and have you talk with me, especially after the last words you wrote to me just before you were killed. I wonder if your feelings, beliefs, or attitudes have changed and what you have to say to me now."

His dad's reply follows: "Carolyn and I died just after Mother, and I have been proud of how you have survived after losing all of us in such a short time. My only regret is that I didn't get to know you in the new life you live and that we didn't get to spend the time we planned in Israel before my time came to go to what is really home.

"You know you have much more to do, Bob. I didn't know it when I was with you, but I know it now. Your real work, what you came to earth for, still lies ahead. Don't fear it. Don't put it off. I will always be there to help you, for that is my major job on this side. You haven't allowed me to be part of your work, but that's what my assignment is now. But only if you ask for it.

"All that stood between us before I returned here is inconsequential, dear son. I wanted only what I felt was best for you, but I couldn't know what that was. Only you could know that. What is important to me now is that you know that I am anxious and willing and able, with better insight than while on earth. Do you want my help, dear son?"

Bob replied, "Yes, Dad, I want it totally!"

His father's answer begins, "Then it is all yours—100 percent yours. Carolyn and Mother and I are excitedly awaiting your call for help and your recognition that we can . . . CAN . . . help from this side. We three are part of your overall team of guardians and guides that number well over 1,000. Believe me, Dear Son, you and yours are well cared for.

"Come for advice. Come for reunion of mind and spirit. Come for resumption of childhood joy and familial warmth. We are only love, and we love you dearly. I am overjoyed that we can talk again. I am always present—as close as the hairs on your head. I love you, Son."

A few weeks later, Bob asked his sister, Carolyn, to come to him. He told her that he was sorry they didn't get to know each other better as adults. She replied, "Dear brother, from your point of view, you think of me as being absent or not 'there.' But I want you to know that in a very real way I am THERE, now and always. It was a sad departure for me when I left, knowing that your heart was breaking with Mom's passing which we never really talked about—maybe because I was about to join her and be together again with Mom and Daddy. How your heart must have ached.

"It is true we never did get to know one another as adults when both on earth. You came back from the army when I was finishing college. Then you went to college and I went to work and then off to France and Vietnam. Trips home were a whirlwind and I never did get to know you or your family. I never did get to know your children like I wanted to. I wish there was a way to let them know that although I am on a different plane now, my love for them and interest in them remains constant and deep and I'd love to communicate with them. All I can do is watch and pray for them now until they make an attempt to communicate with me.

"I think it would be a great idea for you to go to Vietnam, but I ask only if that is the best way to spend your resources, time, and money? I'm not there. Daddy is not there. Our lives may have touched the people there but that was then and this is now. Ask yourself only, What is the best and most productive way to spend my resources NOW?

"Mother and Daddy's things that were with me in Vietnam are now part of the soil of the country. Don't grieve over them and don't consider anything that was there to be important. Our work there was complete for that time in God's scheme of things, although we could never begin to accept it at the time. A new opportunity will come for those people when the time is right for not all have heard 'the word' nor met the God of our salvation.

"Do those things that bring you most joy and fulfillment. Concentrate some time each morning on the God you know and the characteristics of your God, and let your light shine so that others may see Him through the light you share to all around you. Come back to me again in thoughts and words, Bobby. We can know each other in spirit just as easily as in the flesh, if not easier. I love you, Bobby. Oops, sorry for that, but you will always be my Bobby. I love you. Mother and Dad send their love. Please give Mother a call soon."

Days later, Bob asked for his mother to come to him. She had died of a stroke eight months before Bob's father and sister were killed. He said, "This seems like a strange thing to do, but as you may know, I have already 'called' Dad and Carolyn and she urged me to call you. All of this writing, calling, and spiritual communication is not something with which I am familiar. In fact, it is not something our family would have accepted as desirable or even possible. In any event, I want to talk with you and tell you how much I love you, how much I miss you, and how much anything you can communicate back to me will mean today."

His mother replied,

"Dear Bobby,

"I held on to life that night when I passed over and when you arrived I was finally able to let go and make my journey comfortably and easily. You were most important to me when I was with you. I was proud of you always, even though at times you may have thought I was disappointed or dissatisfied with your behavior. You were the dream of a son that I had carried with me since I was a child—since my brother drowned at Playland—and since I met and married your father. I have watched you from your birth and throughout my time with you on earth, but also since coming here where everything is observed from a very different perspective. I can see now that you did not see our 'best' as loving or caring or the kind of parenting that you and Carolyn wanted and needed. If you can accept that what your dad and I did to raise you was our best, it will help you to understand that we loved you totally as an infant, a young child, teenager, and adult.

"It has been a hard road that you have selected and I am not going to sit here—watching you complete the next several steps which I can see and knowing their outcome— and give you direct advice about what to do, where to turn, and how to do it. Heaven knows, doing that as your mother didn't work either. What I want you to consider is to trust yourself, Bobby. No one knows what your mission and purpose are like you do. You know it. You always have. You don't need to take any more courses to complete your work and to achieve ultimate happiness in your current life.

"What gives you most peace? Most joy? Most love? Most inside sense of well being? That's where your work is, my dear son. Think on these things. You have a gift (several, but one significant gift yet unused) and when you discover it and the peace, joy, and happiness it brings you (and lots of people around you), you will be doing your mission, living your purpose, and being all that you are meant to be.

"Dad was so overcome by your 'call' that he still talks about it with anyone who will listen. Keep talking with us, dear Bobby. We love you, we are proud of you, and we want you to experience ultimate joy NOW!

"I love you. Peace be with you, my son. Mother."

These three short communications cleared up a lifetime of misunderstanding and left Bob feeling loved, supported, and complete. Bob's sad memories of his childhood were finally put to rest and his wounds were healed in the most loving and blessed way.

Pets and Transition

Linda's Labrador retriever, Sombra, lived to be 16 years old. She recalls, "It seemed he got 'old' in one week. I felt I needed to let him go in peace. The vet put him to sleep in my arms. It was my knowing decision, yet it was a very hard one. I felt such overwhelming guilt! Had I done the right thing? I kept asking him to come and let me know. I wanted to know if he got to heaven and that he was okay.

"Three days after his death, I was in my bedroom when I heard his exact bark. It was a funny bark, so I knew it was he. I thought I wanted him back so badly that I was hearing things. Then I heard Sombra bark one more time, and I ran to the door where I heard the bark coming from. He was gone, but I realized then that he came back to tell me he was okay and that his spirit was free. He left me with an over-whelming LOVE in my heart, and the pain and grief just seemed to melt away. This was his gift to me, and I know one day I will see my dog again."

Wendy had a similar experience after the death of Cyprien, a Siamese cat that had lived with her for 15 years. She explains, "He was my best friend, and when he died I was grief-stricken. When he died I was not at home, and later I was upset that I had not been there. About two nights after he died, I dreamed I was walking down the street and he came walking up the street toward me and told me good-bye. I know he was really telling me goodbye because we had not been able to say it in person. I know he was comforting me."

Peggy's husband, Bob, appeared when it was time to let their faithful dog go. She writes, "My dog Neemo's health failed to the degree that I knew he needed to be let go. I had promised Neemo that when it was time for him to go, he was to tell me somehow, and I would honor his wishes. One day his back legs gave out from under him, and he looked at me with pleading eyes. I knew it was time.

"My husband had died only a year earlier, and I was deeply saddened by what I needed to do. I called the vet, and he told me to bring Neemo in at 6:00 P.M. so that he would be the last patient. We arrived a bit early and waited outside till the last client left. Neemo was on a leash and was licking my face as he stood beside me.

"Suddenly, he looked away. He went to the end of the leash and dropped his head slightly, as he did when in complete focus. He would not move. He appeared to be staring into thin air. I called his name and tugged on the leash, but he would not budge. He stayed like that for at least a minute. Finally, I tugged and he turned back to me, but turned again to stare at the same spot he had been looking at earlier.

"The vet called us in and I knelt on the floor, holding Neemo's head, petting him and thanking him for being such a good companion while the vet gave him the injection. Neemo closed his eyes and slipped away peacefully.

"As I held him, I felt a hand on my right shoulder, and I felt my husband's energy in the room. I heard my husband's voice in my head. 'You did good,' he said. 'You did good.' As difficult as it was to let Neemo go, two days shy of a year since losing my husband, Bob's appearance assured me that all was well. I had done the right thing, and there is no doubt in my mind that my dog saw Bob approaching when we were in the parking lot. Bob had come to comfort Neemo and me. Thank you, Bob."

Marti's grandfather paid a visit after she had to put her beloved cat to sleep. She recalls, "Tina had been our companion for 18 years, but she could no longer find her way. We even had to put her in front of her food bowl to eat. Knowing how difficult this decision was for me, my sister volunteered to take Tina to the vet and stay with her to the end.

"Just before it was time to take her, I sat on the floor holding her. I explained why we felt this was the best thing. I also told her what she needed to do when she got to heaven: (1) she needed to find God and tell him how grateful we were that he allowed her to be a part of our lives; (2) she was to find Grandpa T. He would take care of her until we could be together again. I reminded her that Grandpa was the one who brought chocolate candy to the kids when they were young. Tina would sit in front of Grandpa in a begging position till she got some, too. She was to look for the man with the candy in his pocket. Then my sister took Tina to the vet.

"One Sunday, several months later, my son, a meditator, casually mentioned that he had talked to Grandpa T. He said that his grandpa had asked him to give me a message. Grandpa said, 'Tell your mom that Tina is okay. She can run and jump like when she was young. She is very happy.' Then he added, 'Tell her Tina found me by the candy in my pocket.' My son had not known about my final goodbye to Tina.

"I just want to say thanks to my sister, who had the courage I did not. Thanks to Grandpa T., who felt he should reach across from his new world back into ours. Thanks to my son, who was open for the message. And thanks to our little friend, Tina, for finding a way to love and comfort us once again."

Linda's dog, Killer, was old and ill. She decided to ask the angels if she had a right to put him down. Here is their reply:

"My child, sit on the floor with your little dog's soul and softly speak with him. Gently stroke him and tell him he will be better. His suffering comes from his diet and his age, plus his environment of being with cats. Explain that you love him and ask what he wants to do. Listen within to his reply. It is

his decision whether to leave his tired body or go on. If he wants to stay, take time each day just for him. His dog physical energy may not appear to be listening, but his soul will be. Every journey must end so to start again. If his pain is too great, you will know. Your love will aid either his new journey or make this one more acceptable. Think of him often with love in your heart and see him bathed in a healing light, which comes direct from God."

Linda listened to Killer with her heart and knew he was ready to go. Here is the last message from the angels about Killer, after he died:

"Your little dog was transformed in an instant to another vibrational frequency. He is free and happy. You did the right thing. Worry not for him. All is well. Yes, we were with you when your little friend came across. Take comfort."

⚘

AN ANGEL MESSAGE: Life here is harmony. Everything is as you have always wanted it to be. When you die, you find your harmony. There is no doubt, fear, or pain. Your work progresses smoothly, and you are busy and happy. You visit with friends and there is peace. All of you will learn soon enough, but we want to bring you hope and something to look forward to. That is why we say these things.

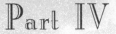

Part IV

The Connection:
Conversations with Souls

Ask, ask, ask.
We are waiting to talk with you.
. . . the angels

Once our loved ones have crossed over, they may or may not come back to visit. Sometimes they do. Sometimes they don't. We have given you stories of those who have had a loving experience, but many people have also said they have not had a loved one come back to them.

In this section, we will teach you how to connect with your own loved ones who have gone to the other side and how to ask them for a message. You won't believe how easy it is to "call them up."

Our primary teaching has always been that you can communicate with your angels. Now our teaching has been expanded. We have been directed to teach you how to communicate with your deceased loved ones, and that such communication is real. Your loved ones *want* to talk to you! Invite them to do so. Simply ask them to come to you with a message, believe that they will show up, listen to them, and thank them for coming and for their message.

Twenty-five

You Can Talk with Your Loved Ones

In the past we occasionally received a message in writing from someone who had died, but we thought *they* had initiated the writing. We had never before considered contacting loved ones ourselves. We were busy writing and talking to the angels, but when the time was right our minds were opened to the ability to speak to souls who had made their transition. Angels, who are messengers from God, are here to help us whenever they are called upon for any reason, including making contact with our departed loved ones. They invite us to ask for their help in every life circumstance, and they are certainly there when death is at hand, just as they are there when we desire to communicate with a loved one who has passed over.

It would happen at times, when we were talking to our angels, that one of our departed relatives would come in to chat. The first time we heard from our parents, we wept. They were so like themselves! Their energy hadn't changed much, but it was sweeter and happier. We were overwhelmed with their love.

Now we have learned that we may call up our departed friends and loved ones to receive messages of comfort, teaching, apology, direction, and love. Deceased ones give us messages for family members who are still here, and they tell us what heaven is like. They are thrilled and happy we initiated contact. It is as though souls in spirit form had been waiting for us to approach them first, and then they had lots to say.

Virginia, one of Barbara's best friends, went through three separate courses of chemotherapy over a 10-year period. Barbara sat with her each time her chemo was being administered. These were pleasant and enjoyable times. Barbara recalls, "We had lunch sent in, rented funny movies, and talked. It was our time together, and we made it nice. The chemotherapy was a reality, but we learned it didn't have to be a gloomy reality. I remember those days as being wonderful! Since Virginia's daughter lived far away, it was my opportunity to take her place. I was able to do the things for Virginia that I was unable to do for my mom because I was too far away when she was ill. In that way, I got to pass it on."

After Virginia's death, Barbara wrote to her, said hello, and received an entire message about Virginia's new home, plus some instructions for Virginia's daughter.

Barbara wrote, "Dear Virginia, are you there? I have missed you."

And Virginia replied, "And I have missed you, child. However, I can check in on you easily from time to time, and you cannot check in on me. Yet if you ask, I will come to you. Time is not the same here. Remember how I used to have such a schedule? Go to this doctor; go to that one? Now I just think or ask and it happens. It is instantaneous. No waiting. Thank you for all the help you gave me the final days. It was wonderful."

Barbara responded, "I really liked it, too. Especially that last day when you felt so well and we could talk."

Virginia said, "Yes, that was a good day. I had times like that so I could be with my special friends and let them remember me as well, and not always as sick. That was important to me. My daughter did well, too. Our love was what I always wanted it to be. There were no past issues left. Isn't it funny that we have to die to say goodbye? Maybe we should say it when we are younger and know that a true goodbye is not a sad thing but a loving thing. It is like I am saying goodbye for now and I will miss you, but I will see you soon. That is how it was for me. It was just for now. Later we would get together again. It was not final at all. Just loving."

Barbara asked, "After you left, did you find out why we were always so special to each other?"

Virginia answered, "Yes, I did. I wanted to know too, for I truly loved you. We understood each other on a soul level because of shared experiences. It was very, very good.

"Don't be sad, remembering as you are right now. Remember the funny things we shared. Please remember those. My last years were of dying, dying, dying. Everyone thought I was dying except you and me. When you think about it, I wasn't dying at all. Not till the last week. Then I was dying. My soul was separating from my body. My poor old tired and sick body was just not a good enough place for my soul to live in. I was a slum. Ha ha. I deserved a better 'house' than that. Ha ha.

"Now I have it—a better house. It is unexplainable here. Remember when I told you I thought my ex-husband was dead? He was. Saw my brother, my sister, and my mother. It is like we get to come together to be happy and love each other and then we go our ways, but it is complete and okay like it happens.

"It is so peaceful here. But not like any peace you know. It is better and sweeter! If people knew what it was like here, they would say, 'Oh goodie, it is time for me to die. About time!' I guess that is why we have such a will to live. So we will not go before we learn our lessons. I sure learned a lot during the last years. Eleven years I was 'sick.' But we both know that that time was when I did my best work. But wasn't I the one? Telling everyone everything about how my body was doing? I should have been telling everyone how my soul was doing. Ha ha. It was doing more than anything! We don't know. We just don't know.

"Please tell my daughter to spend all the money. It is such a silly thing to worry about. Tell her to buy flowers for her house every day and know that it is my gift to her. Tell her I am pleased with my small family. One can't be 'proud' over here. There is no such thing.

"I love you, dear friend. There is plenty of that over here. More than you can imagine, and more than you can understand. God bless you, my dear friend. Your work is helping more than you know."

Later, Barbara learned that Virginia's daughter had not cashed in her insurance policies because she did not want to get money from her mother's death. Virginia's message gave her the permission she needed.

When Trudy's best friend, Chris, died, Trudy had the feeling that maybe she could have done more to help Chris, more often. Near the end, when Chris was on oxygen, Trudy regretted that she had not postponed a business trip in order to spend the time with Chris. But at the time, when Trudy asked Chris if she needed company or help, Chris said no. She was too ill even to see her best friend. At that point, her primary caregivers were her immediate family, and as she became more ill, she was saving her energy by isolating and drawing into herself.

After Chris's transition, Trudy wrote to her about her feelings of not doing enough before Chris died. Trudy wrote, "Dear Chris, I think of my eulogy to honor you and I now wish I had said more and given you credit in areas that I forgot to mention. Also, you came to me and asked me to watch over your kids. I feel as if I could have done more and that I simply didn't do enough."

Chris replied, "You must release these feelings, heal, and move forward, my friend. You did so very well and you have no idea what good you have done. My children are doing beautifully and they are wonderful souls who will touch many. Do not worry about them. My leaving them at that particular time was an important part of their learning.

Yes, I am very aware of their love for me, and it is such a joy for me to watch my children learning to love themselves.

"All is well. I now understand the larger picture, and I don't feel the sadness or loneliness any longer. It is so exciting to be home again and to see my mother and father. They were waiting for me when I arrived.

"As far as my eulogy, you did perfectly, and I thank you for your self-sacrifice in giving that message to the world. You did such a beautiful job of telling people of my love for them and everyone. I thank you for your love.

"God's blessings to you and Barbara. Ask for my help and it shall be given. My pleasure. Love, Chris."

We were thrilled and excited when we received these wonderful messages, but most of all we realized that this was the last link in writing *Heaven & Beyond.* We finally understood that this book was not just about what happened when people died, but it was also about how to establish a relationship with them after death.

We were taught as children to believe in life after death. Now we knew that life after death was true because we had talked with those we loved who had passed over. Indeed, we had learned that love never dies.

Our angels helped us to correct an erroneous core belief, which said, "When they are gone, they are gone." Thanks to angelic teaching and inspiration, we opened to a whole new path. We asked our angels, "Did you say that people in heaven have to be asked to come to us with a message?"

And they replied, *"That is correct. When souls have finished their work on earth and return to us to prepare for the next level of learning, there is much work to do in helping people left on earth. However, we never want to get in the way of the learning being done and therefore cannot freely jump in the middle of a person's process. This is the same as the angels violating or controlling your free will. We do not give input to people who are on their path unless we are invited to do so. This is why it is paramount that those of you on earth must ASK for the loved one to come to you. It is up to you to make the contact. Feel free to add this to your book. Many will be amazed with this information and will feel that this is the secret to opening the door to their loved ones in heaven . . . for in fact it is."*

We then wondered, "But don't our deceased relatives ever come to give loving and healing messages to us when we haven't asked for them specifically?"

The angels explained, *"When you are in the habit of staying open to all the members of your divine team on this side, you are often in an open state. You 'ask' at all times. Ask yourself now, 'Am I connected with my angels and forming a stronger and stronger partnership with them? Am I constantly aware of them in my life?' If you say 'yes,' then that open 'asking' for help is available on all levels. The stronger your willingness to allow them in, the more connected you will be."*

Often there is an "asking" without thinking of it as such. For instance, when a loved one dies, the desire to speak and communicate overrides other requests. Trust that even though you may not know it in your brain, there is still a level of permission given for the connection to be made.

Twenty-six

Receiving a Communication

The Four Fundamentals—Ask, Believe, Let Go, and Say Thank You—are the basis of all of our angelic communications. The incorporation of the Four Fundamentals into our daily lives is the main message of all our books and the foundation of Angelspeake Seminars. These four steps are the guidelines we use to take messages from our angels and to receive answers to our questions. By using the Four Fundamentals, you can make contact in writing with your spiritual helpers, guides, and deceased loved ones.

It is important you be specific as to whom you want to contact. If you just say, "Is anybody there?" it is the equivalent of opening your front door to anybody and everybody to come in and do whatever they want. So it is with communicating with the other side. At the very beginning, pray for God and the highest angelic presences to be with you and to protect you during your contact. As on earth, not all beings are of the light and you do not want anyone to show up who isn't.

Say your prayer, and then ask for your loved one to come to you. When you do, visualize them and they will be drawn to you. If you don't get a message, ask for another relative or an angel. Be patient.

The Four Fundamentals

Step 1: ASK. Ask your loved ones to be with you by saying a prayer to wrap yourself in the protection of God. Sit quietly with a paper and pencil in hand. You may prefer to use a typewriter or computer. Be open, and allow the loving message to come through to you. Breathe deeply and relax, but do not meditate. You may wish to ask by writing something like this, "Mom (Dad, Grandma, Uncle Billy, Maryann, etc.) are you there?"

Step 2: BELIEVE AND TRUST. Believe that your loved ones are with you and that you will receive their message. Let it happen. You are being guided although you may feel like you are making it up. Acceptance and willingness are most important.

Step 3: LET GO. Let Go and begin writing what you know to write. Let the energy or vibration come through to you whether in the form of a whisper, a picture in your mind, or a feeling of knowing. Your loved ones will have the same loving voice you have heard many times before. The harder you think, the less flow there will be. As you practice receiving their dictated messages, you will receive their words of comfort, love, and guidance.

Step 4: SAY THANK YOU. You have received a spiritual gift for which you didn't have to do anything but ask. Simply be grateful for what you have received and acknowledge receiving it by giving thanks to God, and to the one who came to you. Ask questions. Expect answers. Don't complicate the process. Ask, Believe, Let Go, and Say

Thank You. Keep practicing; your communications will get easier the more you practice.

We called friends and sent e-mail requests inviting others to try writing to their loved ones, and of course it worked! Immediately, answers and messages came in from people all over the world. As the word spread, people couldn't wait to tell us what they were receiving from their deceased loved ones.

Celeste received a message from her father. She explains: "As I began to write, tears of joy and happiness, and a feeling of love and tenderness, filled my mind and body. My hands were very cold, but it was easy to type— effortless, in fact. A message means more when it comes from a loved one because you can relate to what was said. My father loved to tinker in his workshop. I want to know more about his invention and will inquire further. The message went like this:

"Celeste: Where are you now, Daddy?

"Dad: Well, Sweetheart, I am working on some of the things that I didn't get accomplished on earth. I am enjoying the opportunity to be creative and to invent things. There is something that you will see in your world soon that I had a part in inventing. Chuck will know what this is about as it is mechanical. I enjoy this opportunity and have made quite a bit of progress in my soul's development since coming here.

"Celeste: How do you stay in touch with earth?

"Dad: We are attuned to our loved ones. It is somewhat like television on your plane. We think about you and you pop up in our consciousness. Everything is consciousness here. We don't intrude, but we do hover sometimes. I know you don't like people hovering over you, but this is nonintrusive. I have been able to help your mother on several occasions just by influencing energy on that plane. She has done well since I have been gone and has set up a wonderful path to this plane. I do love her, and it is sad that there was so much bickering when we were together. It did not mean that we didn't love each other. We were just not totally compatible on the personality level. Please give her my love. We do communicate sometimes in dreams, as I have with you. Everyone here sends their love and their continued support for the work you are doing. It truly sends a bright light to those on both sides. I love you, Honey, and am so proud of you. Bye bye, Daddy."

Patricia received a message from Carol's mother, Rita. Rita's message begins, "Give my love to my daughters. Tell them I am very happy and at peace and that I am very intelligent. They will be happy to know that. I was not very smart in my lifetime. Also, tell them to be happy and not mourn me this Christmas. I know they will be sad and miss me, but I would prefer that they did not miss me, but just felt me all around them.

"I am fortunate to have you to communicate through. I am really lucky, for many cannot communicate as I can through you. You are a blessed soul to be so open to this.

Bless you, Patricia, for your great faith. Call on me if you need me—I can help. Tell Carol to call on me, too. I am always with her. I would love to be able to help with the little things. Tell her to please ask for help because I am forbidden to help unless she asks. It is frustrating for me at times. All my love to you and to my daughters, Rita."

Eulalia sent us a letter about her positive experience. She writes, "I was so excited when you called and asked me to write to my dead loved ones. It had never occurred to me that I could do it. And then it was so easy! I felt their presence and could almost hear the music they were talking about, but I could not distinguish it. It is hard to explain. After their message, tears came to my eyes, and I felt peace and well being, and much love.

"Here is what they said: 'Sweet Beautiful Sister, we are so happy you called on us. So is everyone else. Your grandparents, Aunt Serfina, Lourdes, Mary, and Uncle Joe, uncles, aunts, etc. are all here helping you. We all sing together at times. You need to get into classes of anything to do with music. You will need to get prepared for what's coming into your life. Learn as many different songs in as many different languages as you possibly can because you will be taking your music to different countries. Don't be afraid! We will be with you. Kisses and hugs from all of us!'"

We sent Cheryl an e-mail suggesting she could write to a member of her family who had passed over. She shares, "I tried it for the first time. It was quite a moving experience. I tried to communicate with my grandmother from Canada who would have been celebrating a birthday within the week. She was a very special individual. Her message came through in such a way that I could hear her in the same English/French accent as if she were talking to me. She gave me a very comforting message that included mentioning an angel (by a name that I recognized) who came to my father's rescue one day while my family was boating."

Elena's sister called her one night and talked about communicating with their mother. Elena explains, "I was so pleased. I also wanted to speak with her, because I love her and I miss her so very much. I did not know how to start, so I asked my angels if I could do it. Our conversation went like this:

"Angel: *Elena, this is true. Yes, your sister made contact with your sweet mother. You also know that in a past message you were able to contact her, too.*

"Elena: I know, but I was not sure. Can I please be able to speak with her again?

"Mother: Yes, my daughter. I am here. I have never been far from you. You always will have me close to you even though you don't see me. I am so happy because you are communicating with your angels, my daughter. I know that your father will be able to learn to communicate with them also. I would be very happy to talk to him, too.

"Elena: Mother, I love you and I miss you.

"Mother: Don't worry, my daughter. I know you love me. Remember that I will always love you for all eternity. Your father also loves all of you. You know that very well. All of you have to take care of him more. A lot of the time he feels alone because he misses me. Tell him I am always close to him, and tell him to take better care of himself. When the time comes, I want all of us to reunite in God's paradise. Here, there is only happiness, love, and peace. My daughter, don't forget to pray the rosary daily.

"Elena: No, Mother, I will not forget.

"Mother: Thank you, my daughter. May God bless you all. You are always in my heart.

"Elena: Thank you, Mother. And thank you, angels."

Once you begin to write to your deceased friends and relatives, the experience is life-changing! We find that people keep thinking of those whom they can contact, and the writings keep coming.

For example, Dory has found all sorts of relations on the other side who have been standing in line to answer her. She begins with her Uncle Jay: "Uncle Jay, I ask you to come through to me now and give me a message, please."

And he responds, "Dear Dory, you are a bright one, and you always have been. We see you, Grandma and I, and Grandpa is here, too, even though you did not know him. We are all here, and we are blessed, and it is a great place to be.

"There is a wonderful stream here and I chose to have a cabin in the woods. There are many who come and go from friendships of long ago—even those whom I knew for only a brief period of time there on mortal earth. Though you cannot see or feel us at all times, we are there."

He continues, "Your mother has guilt that no longer serves her, and it would be helpful for you to help her see this. She has raised fine children, and her grandchildren love her. She is a remarkable person in this lifetime."

Dory then contacts her late husband, Michael, who died after two years of marriage. She begins, "Michael, will you please come through to me now and give me a message?"

And he replies, "Gracious as you are, Dory, you have been a light that seems to stay lit through all these years. Yet you know so much more than you allow yourself to possess. Give to yourself and know that you have much to offer those who will come to you. Let down the guards and keep those whom you love close to you. You will not be abandoned but only blessed with more and more power that comes from within your soul. Your depth is wonderful. You are light, and the light comes from deep within. And yes, I think you are cute as a bug's ear."

Next, Dory decides to contact her grandmother. She writes, "Grandma Lewis, please come through with a message that will help the readers of this book."

And her grandmother is waiting to speak with her. She responds, "I'm here—I'm with you—I am happy that you ask to speak with me. May I come to you more often, Dory, dear? There is much that I can share with you, for I am with you and I help you. I seek times when you connect with us in spirit so that I can tell you what is in your pathway, and what might help you with your worries and concerns.

"There is an abundance of love for you. Your husband is a man of true love and you are meant for this. There is no child that you have to bear, and there is nothing you have to do if you choose not to. Give in to your every whim. Your car is pretty, child. It is there, awaiting your purchase. It needs to be in a garage soon, and it will be there in the home that I see you dream of and picture in your mind.

"We can see what you do, and we can speak with you. We have much evidence here that you know of us there. It is amazing when you first get to this side, but the amazement begins to fade as you get used to it. We think that more of you should be aware of what it is like here. You have read some books about it, and I was there at your side when you did."

Dory then asks, "What other relatives would like to come through? Please give me a message and identify yourself."

She receives this reply: "I come to you because I have a message that I think will be helpful and will benefit you and others. There is greatness on this side. You are not even aware of how great it is. The fear goes quickly, for you feel so light, and cloudiness goes quickly too. There is lightness everywhere. The feelings are so incredible, it is difficult to put into words what we remember and thought we understood. Time passes here in no manner that you would comprehend. That is always a wonderful thing, for there is nothing stressful here.

"The person you recall me to be was once a member of your family. The name was from a story I told you. Yes,

Uncle Cecil. You thought I was the dragon that was friendly, Cecil, the Serpent. Do you remember being on my knee and letting me pretend to take your nose? You were but a little thing, and even then, at my age, I saw and felt that you were the child who was there for something that would be beneficial to your world.

"It is wonderful to speak with you, Dory. I love those dimples. The angels kissed you."

Judythe, who had been searching through the extensive work her mother had done on family history, says her message began with a feeling that someone was there. The conversation goes like this:

"Judythe: May I ask who you are?

"Answer: Your mother.

"Judythe: Really! Do you have any information on the Ward genealogy that you can tell me about?

"Mother: You have already found all I discovered back to your great, great, great grandfather, Henry Ward, and his wife. You probably won't find more. I guess I could go and look from here and tell you where to go in England. By now his gravestone has probably worn away, but then, maybe not. I'll go and look for you now."

Judythe tells us, "Over the last 25 years, I have been talking with deceased relatives, spirit guides, and angels. It has been my experience that they don't always have answers to my questions, but rather must look it up in the proper place or find someone to answer questions for them. It seems that all of the 'stuff' that means so much in our daily life means nothing later on."

Several hours later, Judythe's mother returned. Their conversation follows:

"Judythe: Are you here, Mother?

"Mother: Yes, I am. I tried to find out more about the exact location of the David Ward line. Not available to me yet. I have to do some more investigation, after which I shall get back to you. The records are here but unlike anything you've seen recently. There is a large source of information on each person and how their creative energy worked to energize the earth in each place they lived. Bless you and your work. Your house looks nice."

Judythe recalls, "Later that night I received another message from my mother that went into detail about the genealogical questions I wanted answered. Since I was going to England, her instructions were quite specific that I go to Nottingham to find out what I wanted to know. Then she began to tell me what to do with some of her things that I was going through."

Judythe's mother concludes, "All is well here. You don't need to save any of the book manuscripts I wrote from my limited point of view on God and religion. I was way off base. My longing to return to the place where I am now was greater than anything I could put into a theory. Burn the manuscripts in a nice bonfire and let it rest. No one will profit or benefit by my investigations. They were *my* translation of spirit.

"I have now learned that a person's work needs to be completed. The light people emit working on their projects has value to the larger picture. This creative energy holds the earth in place and keeps the earth spinning. It is rather like a treadmill.

"My means of expression was my only means—written from my limited point of view. Burn the manuscripts on religion! They are of no use. Bless them and the one I was who worked so hard at her desk writing them. All those brain cells lighted, emitting energy that kept my part of San Diego bright. Burn them all. Bless you, J.; yes, I am your mother."

Judythe did go to England and to the specific place in Nottingham that her mother instructed her to visit. Within 15 minutes of searching in the local historical records, Judythe found the names of her great-great-great grandparents and the date she was looking for. Her genealogical trip was an unqualified success thanks to her mother's guidance. Without it, she would have looked in Derbyshire, not Nottingham, as she didn't know of the family's connection there!

Linnie comments, "I don't know what I expected when you asked me to try to contact my deceased relatives and friends, but I didn't expect this. I received a message from a friend named Teri, who died four years ago of brain cancer. Teri was a well-educated and extremely kind woman."

Teri's message begins, "Think not with your reasoning, but connect your higher mind with all things Universal, and receiving will be easier. Connect with all things good—infinite love. Trust in the Creator of all things and the angels that they will not allow you to receive unprotected. You have prayed for protection over yourself. Trust in this.

"Your mother and grandmother have longed for the day and moment when you would come to this place of understanding. They have made attempts to contact you, but you were too fearful. All things come in perfect timing. This book and the teachings within will be a catalyst of encouragement to others to make contact with us. We are all working together for the benefit of seeking souls.

"Linnie, take to your heart the truth you have been given. Believe in your gifts. These gifts have been given to you to touch the very essence and core of others. You have been filled with abundant joy to bring delight and light heartedness. You have been given intuitive inspiration and insight. You have been called to be a worker of light to bring healing to the broken in spirit and body.

"Your gifts will help others. Others will be helped to awaken to the powerful beings they truly are—bringing the illuminating light that you experienced in heaven to the earthbound. You are a light worker—a worker of light. It is time you embrace the truth of this. I often watch and am near. Teri"

Daniel received the following message from his brother Alan: "Don't despair. We all love you, even though time on earth was rough. I died quickly to let you know that we have more free will in our life to direct the destiny of our death than we think. It was the adventure I had prepared for all of my conscious life—and the adventure turned out to be a blessed continuation of what I had believed to be a tortured existence. This existence was not tortured, but demanded of me all that I had to give, in the narrow shell of the prescribed plan. You remember how I once told you that I was fearful to move to that place of absolute stillness and darkness called death? I thought that place was an illusion, based in fear, but masquerading as the belief that that was the place of ultimate being? I said it was a lesson of false belief created by hope, rather than by the Knowing?

"I now know what it truly is. I can tell you that fear is but a vaporous energy that is one of the strongest intoxicants of universal belief patterns, only that—evaporating quickly in the breath of beingness. Do not be afraid of or recoil from that place of longing. It is the doorway to the heart, the pursuit of creation. This is all I have to say for now."

Suzanne's grandmother sent her this message: "Yes, dearest Suzanne Frances, I am here. I have had time to rest and I am feeling wonderful! It is a good time. I struggled so much in my life, and now there is no struggle. I left when I could finally let go of my attachments to physical things: money, home, and my body. This is why it took me so long to go. You can see now that all of the scrimping and saving that I did was for nothing. It was a product of the fear that I had ever since I was a child, that there was never enough. There was always enough, but I could not see it in my fearful state, and to some degree I transmitted that fearful state to my children.

"It was all part of a larger lesson of *trust*. True faith is not caring where the abundance comes from, but simply knowing that it always comes. I am in a place where I see that there is no lack, no struggle, no illness, sadness, or grief. I am able to be at peace without the constant overlay of worry with which I lived while I was in my body. It was part of my lesson and a lesson for those around me. I am free to think in different ways now, and it is very good. Tell everyone how grateful I am for his or her care of me."

Twenty-seven

Souls Not Yet Departed

Not long ago we received a phone call from a family whose mother was in the hospital on life support after kidney failure. They needed to make the agonizing decision of whether to keep her on dialysis, or to stop life support and allow her to make her transition. Perhaps only those who have had to make this decision can realize the agony involved. Half the people in the family wanted to keep her alive. The other half wanted to let her die in peace. Those who called us wanted to know what their mother wanted.

When they came to inquire, we gave them a short course in talking with their angels, although most of them had already been doing so. Then we gave them a question to ask their mother's soul. We asked them to write, "Dear Mom, what do you want us to do? We will abide by your wishes."

Family members received a different, but very similar, message from their mom. She told them that her deceased family members, friends, and angels were all with her, and that she was ready to go. In fact, she seemed quite eager to get on with her transition. She told each of them she loved them, gave them a personal message, and then said goodbye. They took her off life support the following day, and she died peacefully with her living family around her.

Shortly after this event, we had a call from Cindy, who asked if she could talk to her father-in-law's soul. He had Alzheimer's disease and had been unable to speak for some time. We gave her simple instructions and encouraged her to try.

She begins, "Paul, if you had all your faculties, and your previous power to communicate, what would you tell us?"

Here is the message she received: "That even where I am is purposeful. Do not think to hurry me to spare my suffering or what you believe would be my embarrassment. I am yet learning lessons or else I would not be here. When all my contracts are fulfilled and I have learned all I can, I will go, and soon enough. Though you may have difficulty believing it, you yet have things to learn through me."

She then asks, "What do we have to learn?"

And Paul replies, "Patience. My wife is having trouble letting me go. To leave her suddenly would be too great a shock to her. She sees herself as strong as she really is, but she also sees herself as one-half a couple. When the couple ceases to exist, she will be lost for a time. I am giving her a chance to rehearse."

Cindy concludes, "Is there anything else you want to communicate?"

Paul says, "I want my son to know how much I love him and how proud of him I am. I have admiration for his drive, his aggressiveness, and his strength, though I would have choked had I tried to tell him these things when I could still talk. Also, relax. Stop the rush-rush. I am okay. I am doing what I need to do."

Like Cindy, John was able to communicate with his wife's grandmother's soul when she was ill. He recalls, "It was early Sunday morning when I received a frantic call from my wife while I was at work. She had just returned home from shopping when she found Grams, her 92-year-old grandmother with whom we lived, on the floor and turning blue.

"I left work and joined my wife and her family at the hospital. The family doctor informed us that Grams had suffered a major stroke, she was in a coma, she was on life support, and her prognosis was not good. All we could do was wait and see.

"Two nights later, with the rest of my family in bed, I went into the kitchen to get something to drink. I opened the refrigerator door and noticed the light was flickering. Then it hit me! It was a kind of knowing. I felt her presence in the kitchen. Grams was there! It then came to me that Grams was not aware of what had happened to her. In the suddenness of her stroke, Grams's spirit was 'thrown' from her body. She had no idea that anything was wrong. Her body was in the hospital, but her spirit was still in the kitchen with me!

"I am not psychic by any means. This was completely all new to me, but I decided to go with my gut and talk to Grams as though she was standing there with me in the kitchen. Mind you, I did so quietly. I didn't want the rest of the family to think I had lost it. I told Grams that her body had suffered a stroke and was in a coma in the hospital, and that she was on life support.

"To my surprise, Grams then did what, in retrospect, I guess any 92-year-old Sicilian woman would do. She got mad at me. She told me *I* was crazy. (I thought I might have to agree with her at this point.) She said she was standing right here with me in her kitchen. She was *not* in a coma in some hospital! I tried again to explain the situation to her, but she completely ignored me. I then told Grams that if she didn't believe me, she should pray to Mother Mary or to her guardian angels and ask for help. With that, I turned off the kitchen light and went to bed.

"The next day I called my friend Steve (a psychic, for lack of a better word), to validate my experience. He told me that I was right in my perceptions. Grams was indeed thrown from her body and hadn't yet realized what had happened to her. He suggested that I or someone else go to Grams in the hospital, match her breathing, get into her energy field, and then communicate with her.

"My work schedule didn't allow me to visit Grams during visiting hours, so I followed my gut and told my mother-in-law, Betty (Grams only daughter), about my conversation with Steve. She listened attentively, and said she would give it a try.

"Sunday evening I felt Grams's presence in the kitchen again. I went into the refrigerator to get something to drink and once again noticed that the refrigerator light flickered on and off. I took that as Grams's calling card of sorts. However, this time Grams's energy was quieter. It felt as though Grams had come to terms with the events earlier in the week. Perhaps she had heard Betty speak to her in the hospital. Whatever it was, I was thankful for it. It was a marked contrast to the first discussion Grams and I had in the kitchen.

"I informed Grams that her family had made the decision to remove her from life support. If Grams wanted to remain with us on this plane, she should give us some sort of sign that this was so. If not, her daughter Betty would be signing the papers to end life support on Tuesday afternoon. If she failed to breathe on her own, she would not be revived, and I told her it was not a decision the family made lightly.

"I then asked Grams if there was anything that she could do on 'her side' to release her body so that her daughter Betty and her family would not have to make the decision. I asked her to pray to Mother Mary and to her angels to help her to cross over, if that was indeed what she wanted. I said good-night, went to bed, and as I drifted off to sleep, I prayed that whatever came to pass in the next few days would be for the highest good of everyone.

"It was early Tuesday morning, around 6:00, when the phone rang. The hospital told us that Grams had gone into cardiac arrest. Her heart had stopped. She passed over. Grams had once again showed her love for her family. Grams passed over on her own.

"It's now some eight months since Grams has been gone, and I am still in awe of the miracles that took place that day. Even now, I'll open up the refrigerator and occasionally see the light flickering. I know it's Grams, still watching over her family. The sadness I felt at Grams's passing was tempered by the knowledge that although she is no longer here in body, she is still very much alive and well. For me, what happened is further evidence that there is no such thing as death. Call it what you will. The stuff of which we are made is eternal."

Beverly G. spoke with her stepfather's soul during his final coma. Here is the note she sent us: "I asked Poppa's soul to tell me where he was and if he could tell me what concerns he had about leaving this world. He told me he was waiting for Momma, who died six years ago. He said there was a curtain, like clouds, that he could faintly see through, and he knew Momma was on the other side. He said that when she came, he would go. He seemed to want her help to get through it.

"Thank you for suggesting I talk to his soul. I believe it helped him to let go, as I kept telling him I knew Momma was there waiting for him. It seems as if they made their connection. He died at 3:15 this morning."

In this section, we have shown that you don't necessarily have to write down what you receive from your departed ones. You can ask them at will for their energy, thoughts, or presence. The message may be deepened by writing, but any communication will bring you joy. As Debra explains, "I don't feel I have to 'call them up.' I know that no matter where my grandparents are, they are with me because I love them so much and their love is part of what made me who I am. They are always with me in my heart.

"When I hear bluegrass music, or hear a good sermon, I tell them that I hope they are enjoying it. Also, I just say, 'I love you,' and I receive great peace and blessing from telling them that. I believe that we should always pray for our loved ones in spirit because they receive a lot of benefit from it. Our prayers for our loved ones are sent like beautiful colorful lights of love that can nourish their souls. Isn't love wonderful?"

Linda's son Nick died in a fatal car accident, 16 days short of his seventeenth birthday. She writes, "No one can really know the magnitude of the pain, unless they have lost a child. It reaches a depth in your soul that you didn't know existed. We struggle every day.

"One day, during a massage appointment, I asked Nick to come to me. For one glorious hour, I was able to hear Nick's voice as it had been in past conversations. I was deeply comforted.

"During another massage, the same thing happened. Once again, I prayed to hear Nick's voice, and I found strength and courage by hearing it. My prayer was answered as I connected with my son!"

Whether you write or not, your loved ones want to talk to you. Ask for their presence, believe they will come to you, let go and accept they are there, and say thank you to God and His angels for making it possible. You can connect!

⚭

AN ANGEL MESSAGE: The only reason you may think you cannot commune with those who are in heaven is because you cannot see them with your eyes. So stop looking with your eyes. Feel their hearts and their love for you, which transcends death and life. Love is always available, no matter which side of life the love is on.

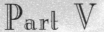

Part V

The Angels' Viewpoint:
Life After Life

Now is the time to learn more about life after life,
for many are making their transition.
We will answer your questions.
. . . the angels

God, through His angels, has given us the inspiration to write this book. Whenever we start any project, we ask God and our angels for guidance. *Heaven & Beyond* was different, however, because the teachings came from so many different points of view. Yet, it was also the same because the willingness of the angels and those on the other side to help us was almost overwhelming. We were very aware of the divine help that was being offered to us. But we were also aware of the attention that we were getting from deceased relatives, friends, and loved ones. At some point, we decided we needed a whole chapter just for the angels' input. As we wrote this book, we returned to our angels again and again to ask for help, clarification, understanding, and inspiration. Here are their messages to us, and the teachings we were given concerning *Heaven & Beyond* exactly as they were dictated. This is their section of the book.

Twenty-eight

Answers from Heaven

Angels love to teach, and the more specific we are in our questions, the more specific their answers will be. You may ask your angels about anything at all, so we decided to take the most often asked questions from our students and integrate the answers into *Heaven & Beyond*.

Q: When do we die?

Angels: *You and God decide how to return to this side and when it will happen. Such an important event as dying is never haphazard, any more than the moment of birth is accidental. God, along with your highest soul's wisdom, combine to choose both moments very carefully when the reason for your living has become complete.*

All knowledge is contained within your "inner knowing" because that is where all memory is stored. As you live, memories are awakened, as they are needed, so you may progress and learn. There is no set plan, but there are definite goals to reach. How you reach them depends on your free will.

Q: Then who plans our life?

Angels: *Life is a time of learning. As you prepare to be born, you choose certain lessons, and desire to deal with certain events and people. You begin to know how difficult life can be. Souls who live on the other side do not have any thoughts of difficulty. There is only love in learning and interacting with each other. This is why the angels are always so excited when the soul is ready to return to us, for there is only joy and peace ahead. A difficult job has been completed.*

Q: What happens when we die?

Angels: *Not as much as you may think. It is no wonder that people expect death to be traumatic, when birth has been such an ordeal! Death is about letting go and allowing your body and your soul to separate. People feel that when they let go they will fall into a void, but in truth, they fall into the arms of their angels and are lifted to God. There is certainly no void. It is the most beautiful of realities.*

Q: Does dying hurt?

Angels: *My, no, the feeling is one of release and painlessness. It is as though you have given up a great weight that you have been carrying, and walked into freshness and joy. No, there is no pain, just the opposite.*

The stories in this book support a message of painlessness. It is in the truth and sincerity of the stories as they unfold that you will find the message of painlessness itself. The moment of death is when pain ends.

Q: Is there really an angel of death?

Angels: *Yes! There are many of us who have the honor of bringing souls home. We have preferences for our work just as you have on your side. It is certainly not a "duty." It is a privilege to do that "work." People who have already died also help us. There is a great welcoming committee on this side to help welcome returning souls.*

Q: Does everyone go to heaven?

Angels: *You go to the place of your highest understanding. You go into your greatest, most illuminated self. As you look around you can see that some people do not live in harmony, peace, and freedom on earth, so when they go to the other side, there will still be lessons to help them understand those important concepts. Learning does not cease with death. The lessons only get deeper because human cares and concerns no longer obstruct you.*

An angel came to comfort Patty when she was feeling particularly sad. Her father had died two months before. The angels said, "You can rest now, my child. Your father's pain and suffering are over. He has been put through much these past months and rests comfortably and whole with us now. He sends you his love and says that you should not cry for him because he has no pain and is indeed complete again. He is happy to be here with his mother, father, brothers, and other family members who have awaited his arrival. They are very pleased to all be together again. They are all looking over you and your family in this time of grief and are sending peace and comfort to your hearts as you prepare for what is ahead over the next few days.

"It is during times like these that you may look back on your life, the things that have happened, the things that you have done, and the things that you had hoped to do or could have done. There have been many struggles for your family over the years, both as a whole and with each of you individually. You have each made good decisions and bad decisions, but through every situation, even when it seemed that something 'bad' had happened, know that it all happened for a purpose. Through each of these trials and tribulations, there was a lesson taught, and a lesson learned. It is through these lessons that each of you has been brought to be the person you are today. We are most pleased with all of you.

"Use this time of togetherness to love each other. You have all done what has been expected of you, and no one should feel any inadequacy or remorse. Release all the stress you have built up over the last months of illness, and go in the peace and under-standing that what each of you did was always for good. Hold on to the memories of happy times. Treat each day as if it is your last on earth. Take time for yourself to smell the roses, watch the clouds, and see the love in a child's eyes as he hugs you. Take time for yourself and the ones you love. Smile, laugh, and play, but most of all, love with all your heart and soul!

"Love costs nothing and only takes a mere breath to express. Tell your family you love them, and make all hearts happy."

We could have asked our angels many questions about the transition process and what happens afterward. But in their wisdom, they sent us stories and experiences so that each person could teach others about what it is like from their own observation or encounter.

Twenty-nine

Near Death Experiences

On occasion, there has been trauma or disease to a body that is so intense that the soul separates from the body and begins the transition process before it is time for the body to die. We asked the angels to explain. Angels: *We work according to God's plan. One of our duties as angels is to make sure that those whose time has not yet come are told to go back. We may also help to heal their bodies, if healing is needed. We will do that in order to help them sustain their life. Sometimes there is a choice for the soul. Sometimes we send them back, even though they may prefer to stay. Trust that we see the bigger picture.*

Here are some near death experiences (NDE) that people shared with us. Snooky begins, "When I was five I had a near death experience. I saw my angel. There was so much love surrounding me. It was more than anyone could experience in human reality. It enfolded me and made my heart swell with feelings of warmth and love. I still remember it like it was yesterday, even after 45 years. I have never had a fear of dying since I saw my angel that day. I know what to expect.

"At the time, I didn't want to go back. I was shown my mom's face, and I knew I had to return to my body. I never told my mom about the NDE because I didn't think she would understand, and might be hurt if I told her I didn't want to come back."

Dr. Victor, a retired psychiatrist, writes, "This is my experience of a near death event that happened recently. It is difficult to relate my story due to the confusion that I found myself in. For several days afterward, I was in a state of limbo, unable to communicate with others. Personal, intimate happenings are not easily described, and only because time has passed can I examine my feelings and let the words flow freely.

"One evening while sleeping, I awoke and felt I was being abruptly hurled into an out-of-body state. My feet left the ground and my body hovered in space, weightless and uncontrolled. Blackness surrounded me, and I was alone. All of a sudden, a bright light appeared behind a group of black clouds, and the horizon was illuminated in a way I had never seen before. All was soundless. As my body went closer, the light intensified, and a clear voice erupted from within the light. This powerful, yet gentle and calming, voice vibrated through my whole body. It asked me to come closer, and my very being responded spontaneously to the voice. As I drew nearer, the light became more comforting. It was awesome! Bands of light swirled around me, allowing me to feel safe. This exhilarating sense of freedom was accompanied with great inner tranquility. It no longer mattered that my physical body was not a part of me. My soul seemed bathed in calmness.

"As the voice grew stronger, the words were clear, understandable, and very soothing. Although I was unable to see a figure or outline of one through the cloud cover, I relished the command.

"The voice said, '*Return from where you came! You are not yet ready. Do your work as previously given to you. This will merit you a higher reward. Fear not! Embrace courage, pray, trust, and all will be resolved. Your angels are your guides. Listen to them. Now return and begin your work.*'

"As I heard the words, a feeling of relief came, then a sense of elation. I saw no one. I heard only a distinctive, caring voice, which completely captivated me. I felt no fear. The clouds grew darker, obscuring the light. Various shades of white sprang from the edges as I was carried away. Then I found myself in bed, tranquil, peaceful, and restful.

"Now that I am writing about this event, I know that it was a spiritual experience so powerful that it changed my way of evaluating situations as they arise, changed my relationships with others, and changed my own sense of self-worth. I believe that peace and tranquility entered my consciousness that day (and my unconsciousness, too). Dreams are not able to effect such a change.

"Since this divine intervention I now pray and meditate. When you make contact with your creator, miracles of healing mind, body, and soul occur. Before, I was a toxic person, and my life was out of control. I am different now. My soul has been nourished."

The angels explain, *"There are more ways to die than to have the soul separate from the body because of disease or mishap. When the body, mind, and spirit connection is so askew, so out of balance, and so unable to realign itself with a healthy pattern, life can no longer be sustained. As with Dr. Victor, drastic measures were needed to 'wake up' every piece at once, to restore stability in all three areas. This happens often, but few speak of it because of their fear of ridicule."*

Linnie's near death awakening occurred after a severe illness. She recalls, "The doctors didn't know how sick I was! I was bedridden with a diseased gallbladder, but the doctors still had not recommended surgery. As I lay in bed, my eyesight was diminishing and the pain was intensifying. An unearthly tiredness began to blanket me, pulling me down, down, down, until I felt part of the earth. It was a chore to lift a finger, and my strength to fight for life was filtering out of me like water flowing out of a leaky boat. I was too tired to fight anymore. That is when I heard my name being called.

"I knew the voice. It was filled with compassion—a love that encompassed me and filled me. It was breathtakingly loving, and it brought tears to my eyes. The voice told me that it was all right if I wanted to let go . . . and I did. It was then that I heard music, a mixture of bell, bird, voice, and instruments. The music was alive and was filled with the same love. It comforted me, within and without.

"Something drew me to the end of my bed, where a smoky, foggy mist was forming. The closer the mist came to me, the farther I felt from myself, my room, and even this earth. Suddenly I found myself standing in a cloud-like tunnel, which revolved slowly, clockwise, around me. It was beautiful, fascinating, celestial, and sacred, and it was bathed in a radiant, pure white light.

"I was mesmerized by the way light seemed to dance off the side of the pastel colors in the tunnel. The colors seemed to sparkle and shine like glitter or thousands of lights, each as small as sand. I was drawn to the center of the cloud-like tunnel to the source of the light, which was so intense it could have blinded me. The light seemed to be translucent, transparent, and alive, and filled with unconditional love.

"I knew this love had come from the same place I had come from. It was home. I was home, and I never wanted to leave. Then from out of the light came a figure. To me, it was Jesus, and he *was* the light. I saw the side of his cheek and his hands outstretched to me. Then the phone rang, and I was back in my room with the mist and the music.

"My friend had called to tell me that she was worried about me. She said I sounded hollow, like I was very far away in a cave. This exact same experience repeated itself again that week, right down to my friend calling me. She will tell you that it is true.

"Eventually the doctors removed my gallbladder, but months later I was still not well. One day, while at a friend's house, they offered to pray for me. As I leaned back in the chair, I somehow left my body. I was lifted out of my body and found myself standing on a lush green, grassy hill that overlooked a valley. The grass was alive and buoyant, and it was holding me up, each individual blade giving me life.

"The music I had heard before filled the air, music that I can describe only as the melody of heaven. And the flowers—everything was at the peak of perfection and emitted light and life. The sky was beautifully blue and the breeze blanketed me, soothing away all my worries and sorrows.

"I heard people gathering behind me, and as I turned to look at them, I not only heard but also saw in white letters the prayers of the two women praying for me. Their prayers seemed to pierce the heavens, going in front of me only to hit an unseen boundary, and then bouncing back in front of me, catching me up and flinging me back into my body with a thud so hard my hair was flung up. Once there, I opened my eyes to see if my friends had seen anything, only to see them, eyes closed, intent in prayer.

"That began a whole new life for me. The previous Linnie had died, but no one knew it—including me."

Linnie's near death experience is the closest we humans can come to tasting heaven and returning to tell about it. Her story truly just begins, because later, with her new understanding of life, she sees everything differently.

She goes on to say, "I was told that I was to love others and to help them on their path and journey. When I embraced this directive, I saw that it was not up to me to decide the right or wrong of anyone's beliefs. All I had to do was love . . . love . . . love. So if you are a Hindu, Moslem, Baptist, Catholic, or a psychic, no matter who or what you are or were—all I had to do was love you. How simple."

We were surprised at how many stories about near death experiences there were in our mail. All are basically the same. An event of illness or accident occurs, followed by a feeling of moving forward, some kind of light and instruction, great feelings of love, and finally, the return. In every story, there is no thought of it being a dream, a hallucination, or an overactive imagination. And, every recounting states that the experience changed their life forever.

Thirty

Soul Rescue

The first time we had ever heard of a "soul rescue" was early on in our angel-speaking career. We received a phone call one evening from Joyce, in West Virginia, who was house-sitting for a widow whose husband had been killed several years before in a plane crash. Containing 20 or so other passengers, his airplane had crashed on a mountaintop in South America. None of the bodies were ever retrieved. Joyce related that the house was scaring her. She told us that the rooms were like a shrine to a dead man. His clothes were there, along with his pictures, his belongings, his room, and his awards, and all had been left as a memorial to his life. It was too much for her, and she had a strong feeling that his soul was near also. She didn't know what to do.

We told her that the souls of some people who die suddenly become confused and don't know where to go or what to do. We explained that he needed help to find the light, and we suggested that she could tell him that it was okay to go into it. We recommended that she pray for him, telling him that the angels were waiting for him, and reassuring him that he would be okay.

The next day she called with great happiness in her voice. She said that as she prayed for his soul, she got an incredibly strong feeling of his presence, and that he wanted her to help him. She told him that he was going to be okay and to go to the light. He went immediately! The other twenty souls who were also on board the airplane followed joyfully, right behind him, all saying "thank you." The jubilance those souls felt moved Joyce to tears. She felt she had done a very important thing. After all the souls left, the house seemed normal to her, and she was no longer afraid to finish her house-sitting stint. The agitated energy of the lost souls was no longer there.

Ruth had a similar experience to Joyce. She shares, "Many years ago I was told by Spirit that one of the things I was to do in this lifetime was to help earthbound souls to go to the other side. At that time I had no clue how to do this, and it did not seem to be an exciting thing. In fact, I thought it might be depressing. Was I ever wrong! Of all the gifts that have been bestowed upon me by the Power greater than all of us, this gift has been exceedingly rewarding to me.

"Earthbound souls can best be described as people who have physically died, but who do not realize that they have left their physical bodies and so have not crossed to the other side. For them, there is no passing of time. Nor do they realize that they cannot be seen by most. Usually they have been taken out of their physical bodies suddenly, such as by accident or war. Many think of them as ghosts.

"Here are the circumstances of one of my latest experiences. I was talking on the phone with a friend who lives several states away, and in the course of our conversation, she mentioned that she and her husband felt there was someone else in their home. They had both heard footsteps that could not be identified. I became aware of the energy of a young Native American girl about five years of age. She had died in that general area approximately 150 years ago. I told my friend that I would help the child after our phone call ended, so I did.

"Since there is no time or space on the other side, I mentally saw myself in front of the little girl and asked if she would like my help. She shied away from me and hid her face in her hands. Seeing that I appeared to be a threat to her, I imagined myself as an image of an Indian woman dressed all in white and bathed myself in loving, glowing light. She then came to me timidly. I asked if she would like me to carry her. She nodded yes. I picked her up and she buried her face in my neck and shoulder. I set her down in front of her loved ones, who were waiting, and she ran into their waiting arms. I watched for awhile and then she gave me a wave and a smile. She was where she belonged at last and my friends' home was now free of her spirit."

Peggy's mother died after suffering a massive stroke in 1992. While she was in the hospital, she was awake but could not communicate or understand anything. Peggy recalls, "After she died, she came to my sister in a visitation dream and asked what had happened. She told my sister about what she had been doing just prior to the stroke, but she did not know that she had had a stroke, and she did not know she was dead. My sister had to tell Mom she was dead. Mother seemed surprised."

Peggy's sister told her that Gramma's mother was waiting for her and to go to the light. She immediately left, and Peggy's sister felt a sense of calm. It was a good experience.

Kim's first experience with soul rescue was in 1983. She explains, "I was working in the intensive care unit of a hospital in the Pacific Northwest. This particular evening, we responded to a full arrest on the medical floor of the hospital. The room was packed by the time I arrived, and CPR was in progress on a 38-year-old woman.

"We worked feverishly for the next hour. However, it was clear that her body could no longer sustain physical life. Her physician pronounced her dead, and the 20 staff members who had been crowded in the room quickly exited—the excitement was gone. I was horrified that they all left the poor woman covered in blood, eyes open, and completely naked. I cleaned her off and covered her up, sending her off with a prayer and an apology for the drama with which her life ended.

"I returned home about midnight that evening. My husband was working, and my infant son was fast asleep. As soon as I lay down, I felt a very strong presence in the corner of my room. It was her—the patient! To this day I do not know if I actually saw her or just felt her strongly, but I had no doubt that she was there. Since I was the only one who had acknowledged her in the hospital, she had followed me home. I don't remember being scared, but I quickly told her, 'You have to leave now!' She didn't budge. It became clear to me that she didn't know what to do or where to go.

"I started racking my brain about how to send a soul off. I asked her if she could see a white light. She told me she did see it, but she was reluctant to go toward it. I then started questioning her about her dead relatives. Yes, she had a grandmother and father on the other side. I asked her to call for them and listen for them to respond. After what seemed like hours (but was probably only two or three minutes), she acknowledged that they were in the room. I told her to go to them and she did, and then they all moved into the light. She was gone.

"I have thought of her often during the years. This was the first of many wonderful and challenging soul rescues I have had the opportunity to experience. If you find yourself confronted with someone you think may be stuck, stay calm and open your heart in prayer. Then fill them up with white light and send them firmly on with love. Every single rescue has a little different twist to it, but God and the Angels will help you with the details."

Thirty-one

When Suicide Happens

To have a life cut off abruptly by suicide is beyond understanding. When people feel so hopeless they cannot continue living, family members and friends are left in an overwhelming state of grief. We wanted to know what happened to a soul when a person had committed suicide. We asked the angels, "What happens when people take their own lives?"

Here is their reply: "*Whenever souls live on earth, they are in "lesson." This means that they have options as to what decision they can make in every circumstance. Sometimes, when the lesson is difficult, suicide may seem like the only option. This may not be the best option, but it is one some people choose.*

"*As with all lessons, there is an accounting, after transition, to see how your life experiences benefited your soul. After death, you are given the opportunity to work with angels and others who have experienced the same situation. You will get to see the lesson as it unfolded. We help you. We surround the individual with love, love, love, for in a suicide, the ending was usually an emotionally painful one. Then we allow the person to see what led up to the event, the consequences of the action, how it affected others, and the possible alternatives that could have been taken.*"

As the angels reveal, "No soul is ever punished. We always respect a person's journey on earth because it is a difficult one, and there are many ways to follow a path. God is love and understands that people are always doing the best they can."

We asked some friends to call up people who had taken their own lives to tell us about the experience. This was very scary for all of us because we had no idea what we would learn. We now know we had nothing to fear, because God and His angels' love is with everyone always.

Chrisida asked Joseph if he would be kind enough to provide us with some insight about his experiences beyond the veil since he had chosen to leave. Joseph had committed suicide one month prior to this request. His answer begins, "Fear, grief, sadness. I am seeing the effects of my leaving, and it troubles me. Although I am still experiencing fear, it is also clear to me that the Father loves me and cares for me. Even now, when I have taken that most precious gift from myself, He cares for me and still has His angels here to assist me. These angels do specialized work with suicides. They remind us that He still loves us and only His love can heal the wounds we have inflicted on ourselves.

"Thank you for your prayers. They mean everything to us. We hear you clearly here. We see you and we see us. We had forsaken ourselves on that side, and here we are assured that the Father still loves us. Lessons of the heart do not end on this side of the veil, my friend. They only change in level and intensity.

"Thank you for asking about me and thank you for listening. Tell Bea I love her and appreciate everything she tried to do. The angels say to tell you GOD IS LOVE. KNOW THAT HE LOVES US ALL."

Barbara Z. didn't know anyone who had committed suicide, so she asked her roommate, Kathy, if she did. Kathy agreed to try to contact her Uncle Ted. Barbara recalls, "We said an angel prayer and then asked Uncle Ted if he would like to come work with us for the good of those on this side who are afraid of what it is like over there. Kathy and I both wrote to him."

This is what Uncle Ted said to Barbara: "When I arrived there was a lightness and peace that lifted me and directed me on my way. My way led me to a place where I dealt with my feelings and the illness that caused me to take my life. I was not chastised for what I did. I was helped and encouraged to see and understand what had happened. I was assigned to watch others on the earth plane who were undergoing similar circumstances so that I could observe how they handled their lives. I was told to mentally learn techniques for dealing with my trials. I now have a better understanding of what I did and why.

"I can't say I am unhappy about taking my life because the way I was headed was only going to make matters worse. Now I have many helpful suggestions to use and more knowledge so that I can cope more successfully when I try the same kind of life events next time.

"Thank you for allowing me the opportunity to be heard and known. My name will be mentioned on earth once again. I feel important and helpful."

And here is what he said to Kathy: "Dearest Kathy. For a while I felt very sad because the pain I felt that had caused me to leave was not so powerful on this side. I was sad because what I had done was so foolish.

"My earth pain was from fear of knowing myself. I was a creator of thought and beauty, but was afraid to use it. Since I didn't learn in my adult years on earth, I now need to learn here and it's harder. But all is well.

"There are no repercussions for my committing suicide, but there was a long time of healing and learning because my soul was wounded from my earth journey. It is a lot different here than I expected, but it is a loving, caring, and healing place.

"I miss you. Love, Uncle Ted."

Barb D. had dreaded talking to her dad because she had had no contact with him for many years. When she did, the results were not what she expected. She started, "Dear Dad, What was it like for you when you left this life by shooting yourself? Can you tell me?"

Her dad replied, "Hi Chicken, I have missed you so much. Of course I can tell you what it was like, but I would not recommend anyone do what I did. Once I pulled the trigger, a big POP went off like a balloon, but louder. I was in the dark for a while wondering what was happening. I remember thinking I had made a really big mistake but knew there was nothing I could do about it then.

"Once the dark went away, I was seeing the room where my body was and saw the mess that was there. I was thinking that someone had to clean it before the kids came home from school, but it was too late, because here Carol came in with April behind her. Oh, they screamed so loud the neighbors heard them. The neighbors came and called 911. I wanted to hold the girls and tell them it was really OK. and that Daddy did love them. I didn't want to see them go through the terror they were experiencing. I don't know why I had to watch this, but I guess this was my lesson to learn for doing what I did. I have gone to them many, many, many times in their dreams to let them know I was OK, but they couldn't hear me.

"I saw how you were blaming my wife and how you thought she drove me to that point. Please release those feelings toward her because I did it by free choice. No one was to blame but myself.

"Once I saw all the pain I had caused others, which I did not think would happen, I was taken to a room by a couple of other people on this side. I got to see my life and realized that it really wasn't all that bad. I also saw the future and what beautiful girls you all grew up to be. I was then put in another room where I saw the way my life was supposed to go and how it was to end.

"I eventually was given work to do helping others that came here the same way I did. I guess I had to relive that part of it for a while. Now I am on assignments and your mother is with me. That's all I can tell you right now. We love you very much! We were always meant to be together and never should have divorced. In our human life, we spent too much time listening to what others said, and not enough time listening to what our inner knowing was telling us to do.

"I need to go now, so please remember that I am here for you. No, I have not forgotten you like you thought I had. Time is different here so it hasn't been as long as you think it has.

"I love you very much. Dad"

Jina had a friend whose husband had killed himself a year before. She wrote him, and here is the exact communication.

"Dear Ross, Please let me know how you felt after committing suicide. What was it like once you left the physical plane? We would appreciate your help so that we may assist others here on earth."

"Dear Jina, it was the first time I felt released, as if chains had been lifted off me. I no longer hurt. I felt free. There was total white light and love surrounding me as if I had come home. Please tell my wife I am sorry this has caused her and the boys such pain, but I didn't know any other way. She can now live fully and I know she'll take good care of the kids. Please let them know that I love them all."

Whatever we thought the messages would be from those who have committed suicide, we did not expect this. And yet we should have known that no matter what life choices we make, we are still loved and that lessons are being learned.

Kathleen F. sent us this note. She begins, "I have read your books and have really been helped by my angels, especially the night my husband committed suicide. I was lying on the sofa, trying to get some sleep, when the whole room became a golden glow. The most peaceful feeling came over me. I could hear quiet whispers saying, '*Everything is going to be all right. Trust us to guide you. We were sent here to be with you. He is with us, he is at peace.*'

"Since that night my angels have guided me constantly. They are always at my side and have helped place me back onto the pathway of life. They have helped me see that my husband's suicide was a very unselfish act on his part. He knew he was dying and he didn't want me to see that.

"It was my religious teaching that those who commit suicide will never enter the kingdom of heaven. This is not true. The angels have assured me of that."

Thirty-two

The Angels Arrive!

Angels are always there. The one consistency that runs through all of the stories we received is that there is divine help for us all the time. The thought of transition is made much easier if you know that angels and souls who love you are accompanying you home during this important event. Here are more questions we were asked and gave to our angels to answer.

Q: Why is everyone so sad if transition is such a beautiful thing?

Angels: *People are sad, because they miss the one who is no longer physically present. There is nothing fearful or sad or final about this period of life. Imagine it the other way. Think of birth. Think of a soul waiting to be born into life. Before a baby is born, there is a contract made with its soul, with God, and with the angels, to complete certain tasks, to learn certain lessons, and to do certain work. The soul's whole life will be spent trying to do those contractual things.*

When the child is around one or two years old, there is no longer a conscious memory of this contract, but the child, usually, still feels the presence of us and is aware of us. Around six or seven, the child begins to forget us, and integrates into the "real world" as a person with work to do and lessons to learn. About this time, the soul forgets why it was born and then spends the rest of its life trying to remember. You are sad because you have forgotten what is waiting on the other side for the one who has left.

Q: I have heard that people see their dead relatives and other beings when they are dying. That would frighten me!

Angels: *Would it frighten you to see your mother or grandfather when they came to tell you how happy they were for you, how much they loved you, and that they have been waiting to communicate with you? Would it frighten you to see everyone you have ever loved when they come to you with open arms and joyful hearts? Just the opposite; you would be thrilled to pieces to see them!*

In a dream, Lorraine was able to see her parents' reunion on the other side. She recalls, "My mother passed away suddenly last November, 12 years after my father passed away. The night my mother died in her sleep, I had a dream that I was in an unfamiliar room. Suddenly, my father came rushing in, asking, 'Where is she?' I pointed behind me and said, 'She's over there.' Without another word, he immediately rushed past me to go get her. That was all. It is such a comfort to know they are happily together again."

Q: Do angels and others come to us in our dreams?

Angels: *Yes, but more often they are coming to you and you think it is a dream. It is difficult to imagine that a departed person could communicate with you, so they come to you in a part of your consciousness that is not fully awake, and in which their communication with you will be more acceptable. They will come with messages, instructions, warnings, and questions. Whatever they want to tell you or ask you will be said. Again, these are not truly dreams. They are communications.*

Q: Do angels bring messages from our loved ones?

Angels: *Yes again! We angels comfort as one of our main duties. When a soul is grieving, we often bring messages from loved ones to help. Very often a deceased relative or friend may want to make amends or to set right a wrong. More often, words of encouragement are sent because the one who has passed over remembers how difficult life was and wants to help you with a loving remark. Delivery of messages is one of the jobs we love most.*

Celeste asks, "Dear Angels, I would like to contact my father, James. Are you able to make that happen for me? He passed over in August, 1986."

They reply, "*Yes, we are here, and we can make that happen for you. Your father is here and is anxious to speak with you. He sends his love in large amounts, and is so happy to be with you. He knows that he was in a lot of pain at the end, and that he wanted to pass over earlier, but was afraid, not know-*

ing what to expect. At that time he was interviewing anyone who would speak with him about death and dying. Now that he has passed over, he is feeling wonderful. He says that his parents, brother, and sisters were waiting for him, and that there was so much love and beauty in the next life he could hardly believe it at first.

"He wants you to know that you are on the right track in your studies, and he feels badly that he wasn't more supportive of you when he was on your plane. He thinks that he was very ignorant and saw life from only a very narrow point of view. This isn't the case now. He now sees the big picture."

Angela had the privilege of watching a woman return to the light. She explains, "Fourteen years ago, I learned that my best friend's sister, Patty, had inoperable brain cancer. I had never met Patty, but in spite of that I felt a special kinship with her through her sister, since we were both good friends and social workers.

"On a sunny afternoon I was preparing for work, doing my usual routine, which included meditating. While meditating, I felt a sudden tiredness come over me that was so powerful it caused me to lie down. When it didn't pass, I called work to let them know I would be delayed. As the afternoon wore on, I felt a coldness that extended from my feet to my waist, and I was unable to move. I didn't panic but decided to go back into meditation to see if I could get any insight about what caused me to feel so poorly.

"As I settled into meditation, a scene very quickly entered my mind. I was looking up into a tunnel that had a darkened doorway at the end. I didn't go through the door, but found myself in a round room with no ceiling. In place of the ceiling was blue sky, and clouds moving incredibly fast against the blueness.

"As I focused, I saw Patty lying in a bed with opaque figures around her. Patty was dressed in a white gown with a veil covering her hair. The opaque figures whispered softly, some talking, others praying, and a soothing atmosphere emanated from them.

"In the center of her forehead, the place where Patty's 'third eye' would be was a golden jewel. As she began to awaken, the jewel began to radiate a golden light. Slowly, but steadily, she moved gracefully, floating from her bed to the floor below. She looked down at her legs and, with one foot at a time, pointed her toes like a ballerina. As she finished, a golden light, bright like a glorious sunrise, entered the room, rising slowly over the walls.

"The feelings I experienced during those brief moments left an indelible imprint on my mind and spirit. The wondrous light was filled with warmth and love, mixed with happiness. I felt completely loved and totally understood.

"As Patty's face turned to this light, the jewel on her forehead began to glow even more brilliantly, and without hesitation, she lifted her arms, turned her body toward the light, and was carried into what I can only say was The Presence of God's Love.

"When I came out of this trance-like meditation, I noted the time, called work to say I wouldn't be in at all, and fell into the deepest, most profoundly comforting sleep I had ever experienced. Several hours later I awoke and intellectually tried to make sense of what had occurred. I quickly realized that Patty had died and that I had witnessed her transition into God's presence. I took notes and made drawings of everything, even though I knew the experience was one I would never forget!

"While beginning my meditation three days later, I was again swiftly taken to a place I had never seen before. It appeared to be a darkened room—round with a dome above it. Through the dim light I could see formations of what looked like wishing wells around the room. Standing around each well were several people looking down into the well. I asked for the name of the place and was told it was the 'Hall of Wells,' in which each person reviewed their life events of the past, and also where they could see what was happening presently with their loved ones.

"At one of these wells, I found Patty. She was with two people I didn't recognize, and they were all looking down into a well. I asked Patty, 'Who are the people with you?' and she said they were her grandparents. As I looked into the well with them, I saw the fast-moving clouds again, and as they opened, I saw Sandy, my best friend and Patty's sister, and the rest of her family, crying. Patty said that their grief was too deep for her to be able to get through to them, and she asked me to give them a message. She said simply, 'Tell them that I am fine.'

"I replied, 'Patty, you've just seen God, and all you can tell me is that you're fine?'

"She smiled at me and then repeated her request: 'Just tell them I'm fine.' I said I would and was quickly taken back to my family room where I had begun my meditation.

"When I finally contacted Sandy, I told her all that I knew about when and how Patty had died. She confirmed the day and time of Patty's death. I then told her everything about my experience except the message I had from Patty. I waited till the end to tell her that.

"During Patty's last weeks, she had been paralyzed from the waist down. On her last day, she described feeling her feet becoming cold and that the cold was going up her legs. She slipped into a coma at the precise time I was feeling the same sensations in my body a thousand miles away.

"When I gave Sandy the message Patty had given me, she dropped the phone! Not only had I accurately described their grandparents, but whenever anyone asked her how she was doing during the last six months of her life, Patty would simply say, 'I'm fine.' Eventually Patty's response became an inside family joke initiated by Patty. One time she said to them, 'So, I have no hair, can't find my way out of a chair, go to the bathroom for 15 minutes and eventually realize it is now three hours later, and then to top it all off, I forget where I am. So, I am telling you, I'm fine. Really, I'm fine.'

"My experience has been a great comfort to Patty's family. It has been comforting to me to know that when life ends, we go home to God, that His love is incomparable, and that, like Patty, we will be 'fine.'

"Thank you, Patty, for letting us all know."

Vivian was alone in the room with her daughter after her passing. She recalls, "I knew she was dead, but I was still praying for a miracle to bring her back. I had even promised my daughter that I would go with her to the morgue because I didn't want her taken there if there was any chance for her to come back. I wanted so much for her to live and to raise her children.

"I saw a cloud or a veil in the corner of her room, and I didn't really know what it was. I lowered my eyes. Then I heard, 'Look up.' As I looked up, the ceiling seemed to open, like a trap door in an old-fashioned home, and I saw the bottoms of three angels. I couldn't believe it, but there were three angels. The outer two, on either side, were as big as people. The one in the center was really big. The three angels stood side by side, holding something. I was so in awe I couldn't move, and I was trying to figure out what they were holding. I forgot momentarily that my daughter had died. The angels didn't have her head or her feet, but there was at least a five-foot span, and my daughter was five feet tall. I asked God to please let me lower my eyes and look at the bed, because I didn't want to miss anything. As I looked at the bed, I still saw her there and finally realized that the angels had her spirit. They proceeded to leave, and I knew that my daughter had gone to heaven.

"My worst fear in life was that I would lose a child. I didn't believe I could continue to live if a child of mine died. I told God that if a child of mine was going to die, I wanted to go the day before or the day of the child's death. I didn't believe I could live a minute after she left. But, at the end, I knew that my daughter was safe with the angels, and I didn't have to go to the morgue with her."

⚜

AN ANGEL MESSAGE: This book is not about convincing you how nice it is to die. You will only know that when you experience your transition yourself. This book is about sharing information so you can make the most of your life while you are still living. There is no reason to fear death. Therefore, there is no reason to fear life. Life and death are all one.

Our Final Message

You think your life has an end much like a book.
In truth, your whole living experience is prologue.
...the angels

This has been an inspirational time. Your stories have taught us and given us a better idea of what we really believe, what our values are, and what is important to us. We have a better idea of the essence of life.

Our perspective on living and dying has totally changed since we began writing *Heaven & Beyond*. This was an amazing book to write! There were so many "spiritual helpers," who gathered to encourage us every time we worked on this book. Since we are aware of spiritual beings and can receive messages from the other side, we knew how eager they were for us to get the book done. There were all these souls whispering into our ears and saying, "Tell my family I'm okay. Tell them I am fine." They were pleased to know that you were going to learn how to communicate with them.

So this book is a gift to YOU from all your deceased loved ones, your angels, your spiritual guides, your pets—anyone you have mourned or said goodbye to. They want you to know they are not dead. Their life on this plane is over, yes, but their existence continues in a better, happier place where God is love and there is a peace and joy beyond our understanding.

We like the following eulogy, which Marjorie wrote for herself while she was ill and which her daughter Sally read at her memorial service. Sally recited, "Once you accept the condition of cancer, you become by spirit and emotion more accepting. You realize you are here by the grace of God and you think differently. The material things are no longer important. Spiritual thoughts, books, and discussions become most important. Love at all levels becomes the most paramount.

"I firmly believe it was the prayers and love, the caring of so many people, plus the expertise of the doctors that allowed me to stay so long. Certainly by God's grace. I must have received 300 cards, and flowers continually filled the room.

"I was able to call or write many of these people when I recovered from my surgery. Some I had not seen in years. It completed the circle of my life and has been closure to a lifetime of friends.

"I believe in the power of prayer.

"I believe in God and that God has a plan for each of us.

"I believe that we have a soul that will continue to live when we die.

"I don't believe in death.

"I believe we pass into another sphere.

"I believe God is within us and speaks to us through other people, sometimes in images.

"I believe we are never alone.

"I believe, really believe, in angels. When I was very sick and asked my angels to be with me, I asked if they had names. Immediately, right before my closed eyes, two small figures appeared, bumblebee in size, with wings, and said, we are A and B and will be with you. I believe it.

"Never let size determine ability.

"I believe in a positive outlook, being nonjudgmental, and having concern for your fellow man.

"I believe in serving others.

"I believe in peace. Inner peace is the most important.

"Love does conquer fear. Love is also stronger than death so I fear not. My journey has been a lifetime of love paying back mentors, and reaping a harvest at the end. A loving family and dear friends have kept me busy, have inspired me, challenged me, and sometimes provoked me.

"And above all, don't ever be embarrassed to tell someone you love them when you really do."

We want you to conclude this book with the joy of knowing that there is only life. We found that our old beliefs, fears, and attitudes shifted, healed, and grew as we wrote *Heaven & Beyond*. We learned that love doesn't ever go away, even though the physical body does. We believe that transition is a growth to the next level and that the elevation of our soul is ever continuing. Our angelic group and our friends and relatives who went before us are with us to guide and support our journey and will applaud our efforts because they know that we did well. However our life turns out, the ending is a birth. A birth back home.

Index

About the Authors

Sisters Barbara Mark and Trudy Griswold, coauthors of the widely acclaimed *Angelspeake: How to Talk with Your Angels*, *The Angelspeake Book of Prayer and Healing*, and *The Angelspeake Storybook*, are internationally known teachers, spiritual counselors, and angel experts. Their *Angelspeake* seminars have been featured on many national television and radio programs, including ABC-TV's *Good Morning America*, CBS-TV's *Leeza Show* and *Entertainment Tonight*, and *The Cristina Show* on Univision, the Spanish network. *Speaking With Your Angels*, a seventy-minute video, was produced by the Public Broadcasting System and featured an actual *Angelspeake* workshop. Mark lives in San Diego, California, and Griswold lives in Fairfield, Connecticut, where they both maintain private spiritual counseling practices.

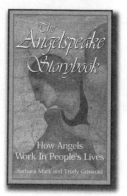